The Jesus Story

THE
JESUS
STORY

By Mary Batchelor

Story illustrations by John Haysom

PUFFIN BOOKS

PUFFIN BOOKS

Published by the Penguin Group
Penguin Books Ltd, 27 Wrights Lane, London W8 5TZ, England
Penguin Books USA Inc., 375 Hudson Street, New York, NY 10014, USA
Penguin Books Australia Ltd, Ringwood, Victoria, Australia
Penguin Books Canada Ltd, 10 Alcorn Avenue, Toronto, Ontario,
Canada M4V 3B2
Penguin Books (NZ) Ltd, 182–190 Wairau Road, Auckland 10,
New Zealand

Penguin Books Ltd, Registered Offices: Harmondsworth, Middlesex,
England

First published by Lion Publishing plc 1992
Published in Puffin Books 1995
1 3 5 7 9 10 8 6 4 2

Text copyright © Mary Batchelor, 1992
Illustrations copyright © John Haysom, 1992 (narrative),
© Maggie Brand, 1992 (information pages),
© Laura Potter, 1992 (parables)

Contents

Introduction

Almost everything about the story of Jesus is surprising. He surprised the people of his time and he will surprise us too, as we read his story. Here are two of the puzzles to be solved:

If Jesus is God's own Son, how is it that he lived a rough, poor life in a small, unimportant country?

Why did the very people who should have welcomed and recognized him as God's chosen King plot to have him arrested and put to death?

The things that Jesus *said* surprise us too.

He taught that religious people were further away from God than those who admitted that they were bad.

He said that getting all the money and success we can does not make us happy. Forgetting ourselves and putting God first brings true happiness.

But Jesus also said that he had not come to criticize and condemn people, but to offer them freedom and forgiveness.

Everyone who met him had to face the question—Who is he? Do I believe his claims? Shall I give him my love and loyalty?

We shall find ourselves facing those questions too. Although Jesus died and was buried, his followers then—and now—are very certain that he is still alive. Through the events and words of the Gospels he meets people today.

Jesus was born into a loving and pious family at the time when the Roman Emperor, Augustus, with his armies, controlled much of the civilized world, including Israel, where Jesus' family belonged.

From the very first, Jesus learned to know and trust God. Mary, his mother, taught him to pray night and morning, committing himself to God's care. She would tell him wonderful bedtime stories of the great Jewish heroes and heroines who, with God's help, rescued their nation from trouble. (We can still read those stories in the Old Testament.)

The life of the family followed the pattern of the Jewish week and year. On Friday nights Mary cooked a special meal and Saturdays were free from work and everyday jobs. When Jesus was bigger he sat in synagogue with Joseph and the other men and boys for the Sabbath day service.

There were yearly religious festivals to look forward to as well, marking the different seasons. In springtime many families set off for Jerusalem, the capital city in the south, to celebrate Passover. In autumn they kept the Festival of Shelters, camping out in tents which they made from boughs and branches. The happy festivals, as well as the solemn fast on the Day of Atonement, reminded the Jewish people of their special relationship with God and of how they should worship him and remember his wonderful care of them down the centuries.

Many everyday things—what they ate and how they cooked their food—had special religious meaning too.

But in Jesus' family they did more than keep the religious ceremonies and rules. Mary and Joseph were kind, loving, good people. They prayed to God and cared for those who needed help. Even before he began school at six, Jesus understood a good deal about the true Jewish faith.

At school, in the mornings, Jesus learned to read the Scriptures and recite them by heart. In the afternoons he would help Joseph, learning the skills of the builder's and carpenter's trade.

Nazareth, the town where the family lived, was set high on a steep slope of the Galilean hills. Galilee was the most fertile part of the whole country. It was sometimes called the garden of Israel. From the hill slopes where the wild flowers grew, Jesus could survey the countryside stretched out below and watch travellers and camel-trains from all parts of the world coming and going on the great trade-routes.

The world into which Jesus was born was one of great contrasts. For Jewish people, the biggest difference was between those who were Jews—who knew and served the true God—and Gentiles, or non-Jews. The Jews were a fiercely independent people, conscious of the privilege of being God's chosen race. Now they were under Roman rule and fretted at the presence of Roman soldiers and officials in their land. Yet the great Roman Empire brought many benefits to the lands it had conquered. The taxes the people had to pay were partly used to provide them with good roads, aqueducts, and public baths. Best of all, the

Romans provided peace and law throughout the empire.

There were great differences, too, between rich and poor, healthy and sick, masters and servants. Most people were poor. They worked hard to earn a day's wage, which would just about buy that day's food for the family. But there *were* some wealthy people, who lived in luxury. Their fine houses were built around a shady courtyard, cooled by a splashing fountain and bright with flowers. They wore fine woven clothes, ate and drank the best food and wine, and were cared for by hard-working servants or slaves.

By Jesus' day, the wise rules laid down by Moses for hygiene and cleanliness had been added to in a thousand ways. Many religious people had forgotten that God chiefly wanted his people to be just and kind. They emphasized the importance of their own rules instead. They despised poor people, who had neither time nor money to live by their laws.

But one great hope encouraged rich and poor alike. One day, they knew, the words spoken by prophets hundreds of years before would come to pass. God would send them his promised King. The Messiah, or anointed one, would set up his kingdom and rule in triumph. All would be well when *that* day came!

CHAPTER I

The Great Secret

No one talked about it—except in whispers, or when the doors were shut and none of the Roman soldiers or Jewish leaders were around. But they were all waiting—some patiently, others with swords at the ready, prepared to rise against their oppressors.

They were waiting, waiting for God to keep his promise. Many years before, the prophets had spoken of a king, descended from the great King David, who would one day come to rescue and save his people Israel.

Hundreds of years had passed, but their words were not forgotten. Up and down the land of Israel, while Roman soldiers kept control, men and women waited for God's promise to come true.

There had been plenty of false alarms. From time to time some hot-headed, wild-eyed enthusiast would announce that he was God's anointed King. It was not difficult to attract followers, especially in the north, where small groups of terrorists were eager to rebel. But the uprisings were quelled by the ruthless Roman army and the ringleaders savagely put to death.

In the hills outside Jerusalem there was a different kind of waiting. Zechariah, an elderly priest, and his wife Elizabeth, lived good and quiet lives, hoping by prayer and piety to hasten the day when God's secret would be made known and God's chosen deliverer would arrive. They were not expecting a king who would lead an army, but a just ruler who would reign in peace and goodness.

Zechariah and Elizabeth had a sadness of their own. Throughout the years of their long marriage they had prayed for a child. Now it was surely too late. But still they prayed for God's promised Messiah to be born.

Month followed month. Year followed year. And God's promise was no nearer fulfilment. Or so it seemed.

A man struck dumb

One memorable day Zechariah left Elizabeth at home in their little hill town and set off for Jerusalem, where he was on temple duty for the week. His team of priests would cast lots to decide which of them should have the once-in-a-lifetime privilege of going into the temple of God to burn incense on the golden altar.

When Zechariah's name was drawn, he knew that this day would be the most important of his life. He was trembling with fear and excitement when he entered the temple building. As the cloud of sweet-smelling incense drifted and swirled around his head his nervousness turned to terror. He sensed that he was not alone. He turned to the altar. An angel of God stood there, splendid and dazzling with light.

'Don't be afraid, Zechariah!' the angel said. 'God has heard your prayers. You and Elizabeth will have a son. You are to call him John. He will be a very special child, for he has been chosen to prepare the people for the coming of God's promised King.'

Zechariah stared in disbelief.

'I'm old and so is my wife. How can I believe you?'

'Because I am Gabriel ,' the angel replied, 'and I come from God, bearing God's message. But since you don't believe me, I will give you a sign. From this moment you will be unable to speak, until your son is born.'

Outside, the waiting crowd of worshipers gazed anxiously at the huge temple door with its bright tapestry curtain. By now the priest should have come out to them. When at last he reappeared, wide-eyed, and stumbling towards them, they guessed that he had seen a vision. He opened his mouth to pronounce God's blessing on them, but no words came.

When the week ended, Zechariah went home to Elizabeth. But still he could not speak.

A message for Mary

Mary, Elizabeth's young cousin, lived in far-off Nazareth, a steep, hillside town in the north of Israel. She was preparing for the marriage that her parents had arranged; she had already made her solemn betrothal promises. She was glad to be promised to so good and kind a man as Joseph. He was a joiner and builder in Nazareth, and everyone respected him.

Mary was looking forward to the great day of her wedding. After that she would settle down to keeping house and raising a family of their own, like every other woman in the town. But then came a day that changed her life—the day when Gabriel, God's angel, visited her.

'Peace to you, Mary!' the angel said. Mary's heart seemed to miss a beat as she gazed in terror at the shining messenger who stood before her.

'Don't be frightened,' Gabriel said gently. 'I've come to bring you good news. God has chosen you for a very special purpose. You are going to be the mother of the greatest child ever born. He will be God's Son, the promised Messiah, whose rule will never end. You are to name him Jesus.'

Mary shook her head, mystified. 'How can I have a baby with no one to be his father?' she asked.

'Your child will be special,' Gabriel explained. 'He will be born by God's power.'

Mary looked more bravely at the angel, though the brightness dazzled her. Then she smiled and said, 'My life belongs to God. Let him do as you have said.'

women because God has been so good to me!'

Mary stayed with Elizabeth for three months. They talked again and again about the wonderful secret that God had told them. The two women and Zechariah were the only ones to know that God's promise was soon coming true. Elizabeth's son would grow up and make everything ready for the coming of the King—the child who would be born to Mary.

'Don't worry, Joseph!'

Elizabeth and Mary could keep their secret for a little while, but soon others must know. When Joseph learned that Mary was to have a baby that was not his, he felt very sad. He thought that she must have broken her promise to be faithful to him.

He decided to break off the marriage, but planned to do it privately and quietly. He could not bear to hurt and disgrace Mary. Then God shared the secret about the special baby with Joseph too.

While Joseph was asleep and dreaming, he saw an angel. 'Don't be afraid to marry Mary,' the angel told him. 'Her baby has no earthly father but will be born through the power of God's Spirit. You are to call him Jesus—the name that means "God is salvation"—because he is going to save people from their sins.'

Joseph was so happy and relieved. He went at once to Mary's family and made plans for the wedding to take place quickly. He wanted to look after her while she waited for her baby to be born. Once they were married, the baby would have a father.

Sharing the secret

Mary's secret burned in her thoughts. She must share it with someone who would understand. She had to tell someone of the joy she felt: deeper and stronger than all the fears and difficulties that the angel's news had brought. There was one person she could talk to—her relative Elizabeth. She was older and wiser, and she was expecting her first baby too. The angel had told her so. Mary hurried off, resting only when she had to. It was a week's journey on foot to the village in the Judean hills where the old couple lived.

As soon as Elizabeth saw Mary coming, she cried out in excitement. They threw their arms around each other, hugging each other as they poured out the story of all that had been happening.

'Your child is to be the greatest one of all!' Elizabeth exclaimed. 'Even the baby inside me jumped for joy when I caught sight of you.'

'God is so great and wonderful!' Mary exclaimed. 'Isn't he kind to choose ordinary people like us? People everywhere will call me the happiest of

'Call him John'

There was great excitement when Elizabeth's son was born. When he was one week old, the neighbours and relatives and friends came to their home for a special party at which the new baby would be given his name.

'You must call him Zechariah, after his father,' they all agreed.

But Elizabeth said, 'No, his name is John.'

Then they all turned to Zechariah, who was silently looking on. He made signs to show that he wanted a writing tablet. When they brought it, he wrote in clear large letters: 'His name is John.'

In that instant he could talk again, and he began to thank and praise God for all he had done for them. Then he bent over the baby in the crib.

'You are going to be God's prophet, my little lad,' he said. 'It will be your task to make way for the greater one who is coming—God's heaven-sent deliverer. The long night of waiting is over. God's day is dawning. Soon we shall all see the bright light of his salvation.'

The village of Jesus' day was made up of clusters of one-roomed houses of clay and local stone, built around a courtyard. Here women ground corn and baked bread while the children played. Stone steps beside each house led up to a flat roof made of wooden beams and hard-packed earth. The roof was a good place to dry fruit, weave cloth—and sleep out on hot nights.

People lived out-of-doors most of the time, moving inside only when it was cold or wet. Stores were kept indoors, but there was little furniture—just a clay lamp and a low frame on which to stretch a sleeping-mat. Light came through the open door and small window-hole. Water had to be carried from the well or an underground cistern, except for villages round Lake Galilee, which was a fresh-water lake.

CHAPTER 2

The Baby is Born

Joseph and Mary knew that the baby Mary was expecting was very special. Everything must be ready for the day when he would be born.

But just before that time arrived, Joseph had orders to make a long journey south. He had to travel to Bethlehem, his family home, the city where his great ancestor, the famous hero King David, had once lived.

The order came from the Roman governor, as part of his plans for a census. The Jewish people all had to be counted, to find out how much money the Emperor could expect to collect from them in tax. Those who had moved away from their family homes had to return, to have their names entered in the Roman records.

Mary knew that her baby would soon be born, so before they set out she put together a small bundle of baby clothes as well as food and water for the journey.

Together they set off on the ninety-mile journey down from the steep height of Nazareth, along the valley of the River Jordan, beyond Jerusalem, to Bethlehem, some six miles further south.

How thankful they were when, at last, footsore and tired, they glimpsed the buildings of the town! Once they reached the inn, Mary could rest for the night. It would be a rough and ready place, but there would be stabling for the animals and space for Mary and Joseph to sleep.

To their dismay, when they arrived at the inn, it was already full. But some kind person let them rest in the rock cave below his house, where his own animals spent the night. There, among noise and smells and dirt, Mary gave birth to her son.

She gently wrapped him in wide bandages of clean cloth, as mothers did in those days, firmly binding his small arms and legs around, close to his body.

There was a wooden feeding trough nearby. That would make a good cradle, especially with a lining of hay. So she laid her baby there to sleep.

Angels by night

On the hills outside Bethlehem, the sheep lay huddled together, under the watchful care of the shepherds. There were many wild animals around—bears, leopards and jackals—and the shepherds were on duty by night as well as day, protecting and caring for their flocks.

Suddenly, the darkness was flooded with brilliant light. The startled shepherds cowered in fear, shielding their eyes from the glory. Then an angel spoke to them:

'Don't be frightened,' he said. 'I have come to bring you good news. This very night a baby has been born in Bethlehem, David's city. He is God's promised King! Go and see for yourselves! You will find him wrapped in strips of cloth and lying in a manger.'

Before they could catch their breath, a burst of light and sound exploded all around them as numberless angels filled the air with music and light, all singing praises to God.

'Glory to God in the highest heaven,' they sang, 'and let there be peace on earth to those who please God.'

Gradually the brightness faded, the darkness returned, and the quiet sounds of night were all that could be heard. Had the shepherds been dreaming?

'Let's go to the city and see if it's true,' one of them suggested.

They made the sheep safe and hurried down the hillside into the town. There they found Mary and Joseph, and saw the baby lying in the manger, just as the angel had said. They poured out their story, explaining excitedly why they had come. Mary said nothing but she stored up every word to think about later.

When the shepherds went away they were singing at the tops of their voices. They were amazed at what the angels had told them and how they had found everything just as the angels had said.

The watchers in the temple

There could be no family party for Mary's child, as there had been for baby John. But when he was a week old he was given the name of Jesus, just as the angel had instructed beforehand.

Six weeks later, Joseph and Mary took Jesus up to Jerusalem. They climbed the steep, narrow streets to the top of the hill, where the shining temple stood.

Like all Jewish couples, they believed that children were a gift from God, and the first-born child was very special. So they came to offer him back to God.

They gave the priest two pigeons. That was the gift the law of Moses laid down for those who were too poor to

afford a lamb.

As the priest performed the ancient ceremony, an old man stood watching. He was a good man who had waited and prayed many years for God's Messiah to come. Deep down he knew that he would see him with his own eyes before he died.

That day he had felt compelled to come to the temple. As he looked at the little family he knew as clearly as if God had spoken out loud to him, that this baby was the promised Messiah. He went across to them, gently took Jesus from Mary and held him in his own arms. Looking down at him in wonder and worship, he murmured, 'I'm ready to die now, Lord. I have seen the one who will save our people and light the way for those who live far off.'

As Simeon handed Jesus back to Mary he said gravely, 'This child is chosen by God to bring salvation. But not everyone will love him and accept his rule. Some will turn against him, and you, his mother, will feel the pain of it all, like the sharp stab of a sword.'

There was another watcher in the temple that day. Anna was a very old woman. She had been a widow for many years and spent much of her time praying and worshiping God in the temple courts. She came along at that very moment and she recognized Jesus too. She thanked God and began to tell others who were waiting for God's deliverer that the baby in the temple was the promised King.

Travellers from afar

God shared the secret of the new king with another little group of people. They were not poor and despised, like the shepherds, nor old and holy, like Simeon and Anna. They did not even live in Israel. They were rich and important

people, from far away, who studied the stars, believing that was the way to understand science, medicine and dreams.

One day they were all bursting with excitement. They had charted a new and brilliant star in the sky. They were certain that it marked a special event—the birth of a king. Together they agreed to follow the path of the star, to find and pay homage to the royal child.

It was a long journey through wild desert, safer for a bigger group. It would be best to join a party of spice traders taking this same route by camel.

When they arrived in Israel they knew that they had reached their destination. They had heard tales, in their own land, of a mighty king who would one day be born in that part of the world. They went straight to the palace of King Herod, in Jerusalem: that was where the new prince would be.

When Herod heard that they were making inquiries for a king, he bristled with rage and jealousy. He quickly called together the experts in Jewish

Scriptures and asked them:

'Where do your writings say that the promised Messiah will be born?'

'In Bethlehem,' they said, 'as the prophet Micah foretold.'

So Herod called the wise men to the palace and directed them to Bethlehem.

'Come back and tell me exactly where the new king is,' he added. 'I must pay my respects to him too.'

As the wise men left Herod's palace, they saw the star again, leading the way. It seemed to stop above the house where Joseph and Mary and Jesus were staying.

Full of hope and excitement, the men dismounted, while their servants unpacked the camels' saddle-bags. Once inside the house they fell on their knees and gazed in worship at the baby in Mary's arms.

Full of wonder, they presented their gifts: there was gold, fit for a king; frankincense, burned in offering to a god; and myrrh, sweet-smelling spice to anoint the dead.

They did not return to King Herod. God warned them in a dream to take a different route back to their own home.

Palestine, the land of Jesus, was part of the Roman Empire, which stretched right around the Mediterranean Sea. The Emperor lived in Rome, but his soldiers kept the peace and controlled the people. Taxes had to be paid to Rome—which everyone hated.

Most Roman soldiers were volunteers. The picture shows a Roman legionary ready for battle, and his officer. Army officers—centurions—are often mentioned in the Gospels.

Roman merchant ships were designed to carry large cargoes of grain and other goods. The Roman warship (in the background) was built for speed.

Everyone knows what fine roads the Romans built. They were vital for the army, but everybody used them.

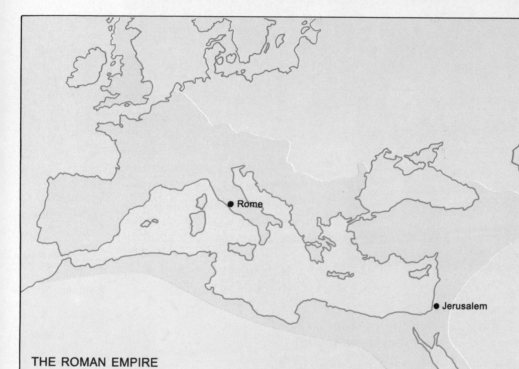

THE ROMAN EMPIRE

Rome

Jerusalem

The Romans were great builders. At Caesarea, where soldiers were garrisoned, they built a giant aqueduct and a fine open-air theatre, like this one.

Joseph quickly woke Mary. Swiftly they picked up the sleeping baby and stole away in the quiet of the night. They followed the road through the plains, close to the sea, then across the sun-baked desert. They were walking in the footsteps of thousands of other Jews, who had escaped wars and famines by going down to Egypt.

Journey to a strange land

Herod waited in vain for his noble visitors to return. He fumed and fretted, then, furious that they had deceived him, he hit on a plan to get rid of his rival. He would order his soldiers to kill every boy child in Bethlehem under the age of two.

No one in Bethlehem knew that the soldiers were marching towards them, on their terrible errand of death. But as Joseph slept, an angel spoke to him:

'Get up, Joseph! Herod is planning to kill the child. Escape at once and go to Egypt. Stay there until I tell you it is safe to come back.'

At the time of Jesus travel was often dangerous. Robbers lay in wait in lonely places and there were fierce wild animals too. It was safer to travel in company, with a guide who knew the way. Camels and donkeys were loaded with goods. Merchants often travelled in litters or light carts. Heavy loads went by four-wheeled waggon. Lone traders on donkeys or mules would join a larger group.

There was a thriving import-export business: frankincense and myrrh from Arabia, fine rugs and embroideries from Babylonia. Pepper, spices, ivory and silks came to the Mediterranean from faraway China.

In famine or war, refugees from Palestine fled south to Egypt by the coast road, or across the desert.

THE ROAD
TO EGYPT

Bethlehem

EGYPT

A Child Grows Up

Jesus was not very old when the brutal King Herod died. The angel came again to Joseph, as he had promised:

'It is safe now to take the child and his mother back to the land of Israel,' he said. 'Herod is dead.' So the family set off on the long road home.

But Joseph soon began to hear terrible tales about Archelaus, Herod's even more cruel son, who now ruled Judea, in the south. So they went home again to Nazareth, in the north.

Jesus grew big and strong, like all healthy boys. He learned many lessons at home and school, and through all the things that happened to him. He could repeat by heart the words from God's law: 'Respect your father and your mother.' But he also did as the law said by listening to Mary and Joseph and obeying them.

Mary knew that God was blessing her son with his love and care in a very special way.

An exciting journey

When spring came to Nazareth and the hillsides were green, everyone grew restless and excited. Soon it would be time to set off for Jerusalem to celebrate the annual Festival of Passover, as God's law instructed them to do.

Joseph and Mary went every year, joining with others from the town and meeting friends and relatives on the way, as fresh bands of pilgrims joined the trek towards Jerusalem.

When Jesus was twelve years old he went with them. Soon, by Jewish law, he would be a grown man, with all the duties and responsibilities that the law laid down.

Jerusalem's narrow streets and bazaars were full to bursting, as wave after wave of excited pilgrims poured into the city from every direction. There were so many things to see and do. But, most important, they must go up to the temple to buy their Passover lamb. It had to be presented to the priest and killed in a special ceremony. Then Mary could cook it for the Passover family meal.

It was most likely the first time that Jesus had been to the temple, since he was carried there as a baby in his mother's arms. He wondered at the beauty of its white, shining marble and gleaming gold. The prophets had called it God's House.

All too soon the week's celebrations were over and the travellers met again to begin the long journey home. The women started out first. The men followed, catching them up by the time they all stopped for the night.

Mary thought that Jesus was with the men and Joseph took it for granted that he was with his mother. The day was over before they met and discovered that he was missing. Frantic with worry, they went from one little group of friends to another, but he was nowhere to be found. There was only one thing to do. Next day they must go back to

Jerusalem, searching as they went.

It took another whole day to retrace their steps. It was the third day before they could begin to search the city.

Jesus would have attended school six days a week from the age of six, like every other Jewish boy. School was held at the synagogue,, where the rabbi drew the letters of the Hebrew alphabet on wax with a stylus. Scriptures were learned by heart, and the boys studied the Hebrew law and its meaning.

At home, mothers taught their children Bible stories. They explained the festivals and taught the girls Jewish rules of cooking and cleaning, and how to spin and sew and care for babies. Boys learned a trade from their fathers.

At thirteen, when boys came of age under Jewish law, there was a special celebration called 'Bar Mitzvah'.

Mary remembered Jesus' delight when he saw the temple; that was the best place to start. And there they found him, among the eager group of students sitting around the leading Jewish teachers. These scholars were talking together, discussing the meaning of God's law, as well as answering questions from the crowd.

Jesus was listening, all ears, now and then asking a question himself, or answering the teachers when they questioned him in return.

The people in the circle looked at each other in amazement. They could scarcely believe that a boy of his age could show so much understanding.

Mary hurried across to Jesus.

'Whatever have you been up to?' she asked. 'Your father and I have been sick with worry, trying to find you.'

'Didn't you guess where I would be?' Jesus replied. 'My place is in my Father's house.'

Mary and Joseph could not understand what Jesus meant by that. But Jesus had come to realize his special relationship to God. Joseph might be his father in other people's eyes, but his true Father was God. His whole life must be spent in obeying his Father and following his plans.

Just the same, Jesus went willingly home with Mary and Joseph. He still did as they told him and joined in the life of the family in Nazareth.

Here there is a gap in the story. The Gospels tell us nothing about Jesus' life as a teenager or young man. We can only guess. But it is fairly certain that, like all Jewish boys, he learned his father's trade and became a crafts-man and builder.

It seems that Joseph died while Jesus was still young, because he stayed at Nazareth, to provide for the family, until he was about thirty years old.

CHAPTER 4

Mission Discovered

In the southern hills of Judea, John, the son of Zechariah and Elizabeth, was growing up too. He was a strong, solitary lad, enjoying his own company and the free open spaces.

His parents knew that God had a very special task for John to carry out. They understood that he must leave them once he was a man, to carry out God's mission.

From that time on, John lived a rough, hard life in the harsh, lonely desert of Judea. He survived on locust beans and wild honey—the only food the unfriendly desert provided. He looked a fierce and powerful figure in his homespun garment of loose-woven camels' hair, belted at the waist with a rough strip of leather.

When John began to preach, crowds started to flock to the desert to listen to him. Some came out of curiosity, some because they hoped that this outspoken preacher might be the long-awaited Messiah.

But when they asked him who he was, John told them plainly, 'No, I am not the Messiah.'

'Then who are you?' they persisted.

'I am just a voice in the desert,' he replied. 'Remember how the prophet Isaiah talked about someone who would make the way ready for the coming King? That is what I have been sent to do.'

Not everyone liked what John went on

to tell them.

'Listen to me!' he thundered. 'The
time is coming for God to take action. If
a tree doesn't bear fruit, you cut it down.
In the same way, God will judge you, if
you don't begin to bear the fruit of
goodness and justice in your lives.'

As John spoke, they began to see that
they had disobeyed God and were living
greedy and self-satisfied lives. Many of
them were truly sorry and told him so.

'Then be baptized,' John told them,
'as a sign that you have changed your
mind and will change your ways. Then
you will be ready for God's King when
he comes.'

John made his base at a shallow ford of
the River Jordan. The water there was
deep and calm enough for him to baptize
his followers, by dipping them in the
river. The Jews had many kinds of
religious washing: it reminded them that
God looked for 'clean' hearts and lives in
his people. They understood that John's
baptism was a vivid way of saying that
they were sorry and would change their
ways.

John spoke fearlessly to the rich and
powerful Jewish leaders, who came to
hear him too.

'You are like desert snakes that slide
away under the rocks,' he told them.
'But God knows your hearts! Being
religious and saying that you belong to
God's chosen nation won't save you
from God's punishment. Change your
minds and change your ways!

'Listen!' he went on. 'There is
someone coming who is far more
important than I am. I'm not even good
enough to kneel down and unfasten his
sandals! He will know you through and
through and he is the one who will sort
out the good from the bad.'

Although John spoke so confidently

about the coming Messiah, he still did not know who he was. But God had given him this sign:

'When the man of my choice comes, you will recognize him. You will see my Spirit come upon him, like a dove.'

One day, John saw Jesus, his relative, among the crowd that flocked to him.

'I want you to baptize me,' Jesus said. But John knew that Jesus was not like the rest. He was good. He did not need to confess his sins and change his ways.

'I am not good enough to baptize you,' he told Jesus.

But Jesus insisted: 'I want to do everything that God is asking his people to do.'

So, a little unwillingly, John agreed. As soon as Jesus came up out of the water, John saw the promised sign. God's Spirit came to rest gently but powerfully on Jesus. At the same moment Jesus heard a voice, speaking clearly to him. He knew that it was God who said, 'You are my own dear son. I am delighted with you!'

Choices

Immediately after he had been baptized, God's Spirit compelled Jesus to go into the desert, far from the crowds and from any sign of human life. There was nothing to eat and only wild animals for company.

Jesus needed time to think and to be alone with God. He must discover how God wanted him to carry out his mission as Messiah.

There were many sayings in the Jewish Scriptures about the coming King. Some spoke of a conqueror and deliverer, who would reign, like King David, and set up another golden age for Israel.

Plenty of patriotic Jews were looking for that kind of Messiah, who would organize an army, send the Roman forces packing, and be crowned king in Jerusalem.

But the words God spoke at his baptism reminded Jesus of another line of thought in Old Testament writing. The prophet Isaiah described God's perfect Servant, who would be despised and, in the end, would suffer and die for his people's sins. God had called him, 'my chosen one, in whom I take delight.'

Jesus was discovering God's destiny for him: he must serve God by suffering before he could be the conquering king. He would win his battle by accepting death, not by brandishing a sword or leading an army.

After weeks of fasting, Jesus was hungry and exhausted. There was no shade from the remorseless heat of the sun by day, and no protection from the cold at night. Then Satan, the Evil One, began to whisper clever and persuasive temptations, trying to cast doubts on God's plans for Jesus.

'You're hungry,' he reminded Jesus, 'but that's no problem if you really are God's Son. Look at these round stones: one word from you will turn them into fresh-baked loaves!'

Jesus knew that was true. If he wished, he could provide food for himself and any number of hungry people. But his answer was firm.

'No! The Scripture says that men and women cannot survive on food alone. We need God's words. They are our real food.'

Next, Satan made all the glittering thrones and cities of the world pass before his mind's eye, in an instant of time.

'Just think,' he whispered. 'All these fine cities belong to me, and I can give them to you. I can and I will—if you kneel down and worship me.'

'The Scriptures say that we must worship God and no one else,' Jesus replied.

Then Satan took Jesus, in imagination, to the topmost point of the shining temple building.

'Why not throw yourself down?' he asked. 'Think of the sensation when the crowds find you quite unhurt! Remember that the Scripture says, "God will order his angels to take good care of you so that not even your feet will be hurt on the stones."'

But Jesus knew it was not God's way for him to draw the crowds by some spectacular miracle.

'The Scripture also says that it is wrong to put God's power and goodness to the test,' he told Satan.

Satan tried every possible way to make Jesus turn from God's chosen course: to be a different kind of Messiah. When Jesus resisted all his temptations, he left him in peace for a little while.

Before Jesus left the desert to begin his mission of teaching and healing and preaching the Good News, he had accepted God's plan for him. He would be the Servant King.

'Follow him!'

Some of the people who flocked to hear John preach stayed to become his followers. He taught them and told them more about the coming King.

One day, two of them were standing close to John when Jesus walked by.

'There he is!' John shouted out. 'He's the one I've been telling you about. He is much greater than I am. I may have been born before he was, but he existed before I was created.'

The next time John saw Jesus, he said something even stranger to his followers.

'Look at him!' he said wonderingly. 'He is God's Lamb—the one who will bear the weight of the world's sin.'

The two friends left John and hurried after Jesus. They wanted to get to know this extraordinary stranger for themselves. They went with him and spent the time till darkness fell talking and listening to him.

One of them, Andrew, ran to find his brother, Simon. He wanted to introduce him to Jesus too.

John was not jealous that his disciples had begun to leave him to listen to Jesus instead.

'Jesus is like the bridegroom,' he explained. 'He is the one the bride belongs to. I'm just like the best man, standing by and happy to hear the bridegroom's voice. I want him to become greater and greater, while I gradually fade out of the picture.'

Parents arranged marriages for their children in Jesus' day, and the bridegroom's father had to pay the bride's father a dowry for his daughter. Some of the coins were often made into a circle which the woman attached to her headdress.

The marriage is agreed at a betrothal ceremony: promises are made, rings exchanged, and the bride-price paid. The wedding will take place in a year or so, when the bridegroom has the home ready and the bride has made her wedding-clothes. ▼

The wedding is a great occasion. The bridegroom goes to the bride's house to fetch her home. It will probably be dark when he arrives. Excited attendants are waiting with lamps lit, and they all return in procession, singing and dancing. ▼

Bride and groom sit under a canopy at the wedding feast, while everyone enjoys the food and wine. The celebrations will last a week!

CHAPTER 5

Mission Begun

Jesus and some of his new friends were invited to a wedding. It was to be held at a town called Cana, not far from Nazareth. His mother, Mary, was also one of the guests.

By the time they arrived, the week-long feast was in full swing and the guests were having a wonderful time. But the bridegroom and his parents were looking anxious and unhappy. Mary was close to the family and knew what was worrying them. She hurried to tell Jesus.

'They've run out of wine! Please do something!' she begged him.

Not having enough to give the guests was a terrible disgrace. The whole celebration would be spoiled.

But Jesus shook his head gently. 'I must do God's work in *God's* time, not yours,' he told her.

Mary was not upset. She just whispered to the servants, 'Mind you do whatever Jesus tells you.'

Then Jesus went across to the worried little knot of servants. He pointed to the huge stone jars that had held the water for the many kinds of washing ordered by Jewish law.

'Refill those pots with water,' he told them, 'then pour some of it out and take it to the best man.'

The servants hurried to do as he said. They filled the great jars to the brim, then drew some off to take to the top table.

The best man took one drink, then smacked his lips with pleasure. 'This is first-class wine!' he exclaimed, not knowing where it came from. Then he turned to the bridegroom and said, 'Most people serve their best wine first, and leave the cheap stuff till later. But

you have left the best till last!'

Soon all the guests were enjoying the good wine, without knowing its secret. But the servants knew. And Jesus' new friends had seen everything that had happened. They knew that Jesus must be someone very special. He could change water into wine. And he could change people's lives too. He was giving them peace in place of worry, turning sadness into joy.

Behind bars

John the Baptist not only preached to the crowds of ordinary people who came to him, he spoke just as bravely and honestly to the king himself. Herod Antipas was ruler of Galilee under the Romans, and one of the sons of Herod the Great, the king who had tried to kill the baby Jesus.

'You broke God's laws when you stole your brother's wife from him and married her yourself,' John told Herod. The king was outraged and his new wife, Herodias, was even more furious. So Herod gave orders for John to be arrested and thrown deep into the dungeon of his fortress castle. Instead of the wide open spaces of the desert, John had to endure the foul stench of a dark, underground cell, where he was chained to the enclosing walls.

Sometimes Herod would send for John. He felt compelled to listen to what he had to say, even though it frightened and upset him. He realized, too, that John was a good man, so he kept him safe from Herodias, who was out for John's blood.

Not welcome

After John had been thrown into prison, Jesus set out to preach and teach. He began in his own home town of

Nazareth, telling everyone the good news about God's kingdom.

One Sabbath he went to the synagogue service, where his parents had taken him since he was a small boy. The leader handed him a scroll of Scripture and invited him to read and speak.

Jesus chose a passage from one of Isaiah's poems about God's perfect Servant, and read out:

'The Spirit of the Lord is upon me,
because he has chosen me to bring
   good news to the poor.
He has sent me to proclaim liberty
   to the captives
and recovery of sight to the blind;
to set free the oppressed
and announce that the time has
   come
when the Lord will save his people.'

41

Jesus rolled up the scroll again and handed it back.

All eyes were fixed on him as he said, 'This very day Isaiah's words have come true.'

The congregation was astonished. A little ripple of indignation ran around the synagogue. Was this local lad saying that he was God's promised Servant?

'He's a good preacher,' some of them admitted. But others muttered darkly, 'Who does he think he is? We all know he's only Joseph's son!'

'I can tell you this,' Jesus said, answering their whispered complaints, 'every prophet who has ever lived has been despised by his own people. Think of the great Elijah! There were plenty of widows living in Israel in his time, but he was sent to one who lived outside the country. In Elisha's day there were plenty of Israelites suffering from skin diseases, but the only one Elisha cured was a Syrian!'

By this time the people were furious. How dare this young upstart say that God's prophets were better treated by foreigners than by God's chosen people!

They sprang to their feet and rushed at Jesus, then half-marched, half-

dragged him out of the building and up to the top of the hill outside the town. They would throw him over the cliff and be done with him and his talk. But while they were fuming and raging, Jesus walked calmly through the middle of the mob and went on his way.

A day of surprises

That Sabbath began like any other in the lakeside town of Capernaum.

But when the townspeople went to synagogue they found there was a new preacher. It was Jesus, the young teacher from Nazareth. And what a sermon he preached! He did not quote other teachers' views, as the scribes did, but told them straight out what God said.

Suddenly, while he was speaking, a piercing scream shattered the quiet, and a hoarse voice cried out, 'What do you want, Jesus of Nazareth? I know who you are—you are God's holy messenger!'

Everyone turned to look at the wild figure who had come in the door and was lurching towards Jesus. Jesus spoke clearly and firmly—not to the man, but to the wicked spirit which he knew was making him behave this way: 'Be silent, you evil spirit! Come out of the man!'

The man shook violently and gave one last long scream. Then he lay quite still, his wild look gone.

'This man is unbelievable!' they all agreed. 'He can preach like no one else can *and* he can order evil spirits to do as he tells them!'

At Simon's house

After the service, Jesus went home with Simon and Andrew, who had been followers of John the Baptist. Their friends James and John went with them too. When they came into the courtyard, Simon's wife was waiting for them anxiously. She led them into the house, where her mother lay tossing and moaning on her sleeping-mat, with a high fever.

Jesus went straight to her, took her hot hand in his and gently helped her up. Immediately the fever died down. She felt cool and well and strong. She got to her feet, beaming, then hurried off to get them water for washing and food to eat.

The whole of Capernaum was buzzing now with talk of the new preacher and healer. As the sun went down over the lake, and the Sabbath drew to a close, a trickle of people began to collect in the open space outside Simon's house. The trickle soon became a crowd, as people with every kind of illness and disability waited for Jesus to come out and make them better.

Jesus healed those whose bodies were sick and others whose minds were tormented by evil spirits. The demons recognized Jesus as God's Son, the Messiah, but he would not let them say so. That was a secret.

A soldier under orders

Capernaum soon became Jesus' base and Peter's house his home.

One day a Roman centurion came up to him in the street. 'Sir,' he begged, 'will you help me? My servant is very ill. He can't move and he's in terrible pain.'

Some of the Jewish leaders of the town joined in: 'Please help this officer,' they said. 'He's been very good to us, even though he is a Roman. He even paid

for our synagogue to be built.'

Jesus turned at once to go with him to his quarters, but the centurion stopped him. 'You are too good to come inside my house,' he told Jesus. 'Just give the command and my servant will be healed. I understand, because I too am a person in command. I take orders from my superiors and then I tell my men what to do. I have only to say the word and I am instantly obeyed.'

Jesus was amazed that this Roman soldier could trust him so completely.

'None of the Jewish people has shown faith like this in me,' he told the people who were following him. Then he looked at the officer and said, 'Go home. You will find your servant fit and well again, as you believed he would be.'

Some of the centurion's men hurried back to the officer's quarters and found his servant completely well.

CHAPTER 6

Friends of Jesus

Jesus picked his way across the stony shore of the lake. A ragged bunch of people—men and women, boys and girls—tagged along behind him. Some skipped and ran, while others limped and struggled to keep up. Everyone wanted to get close to the wonderful new teacher.

The four fishermen

Jesus walked towards two fishing-boats, hauled onto the beach after a night's fishing. He looked thoughtfully at the familiar faces of the four fishermen who were busy about their daytime duties. James and John were sitting in their boat, with Zebedee their father, carefully mending the torn nets. Nearer at hand, Simon and Andrew were wading through the shallow water, trailing a net between them.

Jesus called to them, first, 'Come with me!'

The brothers threw down their net and ran to Jesus. Then Jesus beckoned to James and John: 'Follow me!' he called out. They left Zebedee in the boat and joined Jesus.

They were ready to leave their homes and their jobs, if he asked them to, and to follow Jesus wherever he might go.

Jesus looked at the crowd that was growing larger by the minute, jostling and pushing to get within earshot, in spite of the efforts of the broad-shouldered fishermen to clear a space around him.

Then Jesus climbed into Simon's boat and asked him to give it a push into

the water. From there, he would be seen by the whole crowd and his voice would carry over the water, so that even those at the very back could hear.

'Listen!' he told them. 'The moment has come for God's reign to begin. Change your minds—and change your ways: believe the Good News!'

Jesus did not preach dull sermons. He explained what he had to say in stories. Some did not bother to think what the stories meant, but others listened hard and began to understand and do as Jesus said.

When he had finished talking, Jesus said to Simon, 'Push the boat further out and let your nets down for a catch.'

'Master,' Simon said, 'it's no good doing that. We fished all night long and didn't catch anything, so we won't catch any in the day!' But something made him change his mind. 'All right, if you say so, Master. We'll have a try,' he told Jesus.

The moment they let down the nets, the fish began to stream into them, flashing and gleaming in the sunshine. Soon the nets were full to breaking-point.

'Come on!' they shouted to James and John. 'Give us a hand!' Even then they thought that the weight of the fish might sink both their boats.

Simon waded ashore, rushed up to Jesus and threw himself down in front of him. 'Master!' he gasped. 'I'm a bad lot—not good enough to be anywhere near you!'

The other three crowded around

Jesus too, as amazed as Simon at what had happened.

Jesus looked at them all affectionately. 'Don't be afraid,' he said. 'Instead of catching fish, I'm going to teach you to catch people, to fish for others and draw them into God's kingdom!'

When they had dragged their boats onto the beach, they set off, without one backward look, to follow Jesus wherever he went.

Call to the tax man

Matthew was busy in his tax office close to the road into Capernaum. He collected the duty that had to be paid to Herod on all goods coming in or going out of his province. Like all tax collectors at that time, Matthew added a good margin of profit for himself.

He had heard all the talk about Jesus. But he did not expect Jesus to include tax collectors in the Good News he was preaching. All the Jewish people hated and despised them and treated them as outsiders.

Then, one day, Jesus stopped outside Matthew's place of work: 'Follow me,' he said.

Matthew could scarcely believe his ears. It was too good to be true. Jesus had chosen *him*. At once, he put aside his documents and accounts, and gladly followed Jesus.

The inner circle

Out of the many people who followed him, Jesus planned to choose a small, close group. They would stay with him and learn from him, then help him spread the Good News up and down the country. When the time came he stayed up all night, asking God to help him choose the right ones.

Next day, he picked twelve. He called them apostles, which means those who are sent.

There were the brothers, Simon Peter and Andrew, and James and John, all fishermen; Matthew, the tax collector; Philip, who came from the nearby lake town of Bethsaida; Nathanael from Cana; another Simon, who had belonged

*Jesus never pretended that it was easy to be his
disciple. He pointed out the difficulties and encouraged
people to think first before following him.*

THE STORY OF THE MAN WHO BUILT A TOWER

There was once a man who planned to build a splendid tower. Plans
were drawn up and the builders began work.

But the enthusiastic builder had forgotten one thing. He hadn't sat
down beforehand and worked out how much money the project would
cost. So when he could not pay for any more materials or afford the
workmen's wages, he had to call a halt.

Everyone who saw the half-finished tower had a good laugh about
the man who began to build but forgot to count the cost.

THE STORY OF THE KING WHO WENT TO WAR

Imagine that you are a king. You get news that an enemy is marching
towards your borders, so you want to lead your army into battle
against him.

But you have only ten thousand soldiers and your enemy has twenty
thousand. If you are wise, you will sit down first and work out a strategy.
Are you able, with your smaller army, to defeat him? If not, you had
better send messengers to meet him before he arrives and ask him for
terms of peace.

*'Think about that,' Jesus told his listeners. 'You
must count the cost of being my disciple before you decide to follow me. It will cost you everything you
have.'*

to a daredevil group of Jewish freedom fighters; Thomas, one of twins; another James, whose father's name was Alphaeus; Judas, sometimes called Thaddaeus, and Judas Iscariot.

Jesus had special names for some of his friends. He nicknamed James and John 'The Thunderers'.

When he first met Simon the fisherman, he told him: 'Your name is going to be Peter—a Rock!' It would be a long time before Peter began to live up to his new name.

The family at Bethany

When Jesus visited Jerusalem, he used to stay with a special family of friends, who lived in Bethany, a village near the city. There were two sisters, Martha and Mary, and their brother Lazarus.

One day, when Jesus called with his friends, Martha rushed around, preparing a special meal for them all.

She grew hotter and hotter and more and more bothered as she tried to cook so many dishes single-handed. At last she could bear it no longer.

She went across to where Jesus sat, talking and answering the questions of the eager group around him. Martha pointed accusingly at her sister Mary, who was one of the circle.

'Tell Mary to give me a hand in the kitchen, Lord,' she demanded. 'Don't you care that she's left me to do everything on my own?'

Jesus looked up at Martha's flustered face and put a kind hand on her arm: 'Martha, dear,' he said, 'don't be bothered. There is no need to put on a big spread. What matters most is learning about God while you have the chance. It would not be right for me to send Mary back to the kitchen. She's chosen the most important thing to do.'

'I'd like to follow you!'

Many people felt drawn to Jesus. They thought they would like to be his disciples too. Some of the women could not leave their husbands and children, but wealthy ones, like Susanna and Joanna (whose husband was employed at Herod's court), were able to help in other ways. They gave Jesus and the Twelve money for food and clothes. Sometimes they prepared meals for them.

Others were free to travel with Jesus, like Mary from Magdala. Jesus had healed her when she was very sick in body and mind.

Others who asked to be Jesus' followers were not prepared to pay the price of putting him first. Jesus always reminded them what it would cost.

'I'll follow you to the ends of the earth!' one man told him enthusiastically.

'Have you thought what that really means?' Jesus asked him. 'The fox has his hole, birds have their nests, but I, the Son of man, have nowhere to call my own home, nowhere to sleep at nights.'

Then Jesus gave a searching look at all his would-be followers:

'When the farmer starts to plough a field he keeps his eyes fixed on the far end of the furrow,' he told them. 'Anyone who begins to follow me but keeps looking back with longing at the old, easy life, is not fit for the kingdom of God.'

THE STORY OF
The Farmer's Crops

There was once a farmer who set out to sow his seed. He walked the length and breadth of his field, scattering handfuls from his seed-bag as he went.

Some fell on the path, where the earth was panned down by the feet of passersby. That seed could not sink into the soil, so it was soon gobbled up by the birds.

Some seed fell on thin soil, which barely covered the rocks beneath. It sprouted quickly, but its roots could not go deep, so the small plants soon withered and died.

Some seeds fell into the thorn bushes that bordered the field. They grew, but the thorns soon choked them.

But some seed fell on good, fertile soil. It sprouted, grew tall and produced a good harvest of grain.

'Use your ears and listen!' Jesus ended.

When the crowds had gone home, Jesus' disciples asked: 'Why do you use stories to explain about God and his kingdom? And what did that story mean?'

'The good news about God's kingdom is a secret,' Jesus explained, 'kept for those willing to listen and obey. Parables keep the truth from idle hearers but make it plainer to those who really want to understand.

'This is what the story means. The seed is God's message, coming to many different listeners. Some, like the hard path, are hard-hearted. God's word cannot sink in. Others, like the rocky soil, do not let God's word go deep. When things get tough they do not go on living for God. Others, like the seed among thorns, receive what God says, but worries and money-making and selfishness crowd out God's word.

'But some are like the good soil. They hear God's word and take the message deep into their hearts. They understand and obey what God says.'

Palestine, the country where Jesus lived, has fertile plains and valleys, rocky hills—and desert too. The summer is long, hot and dry. Water is scarce, so spring and autumn rains are vital.

The farmer prepared and sowed the ground in winter and early spring. Flax (for linen) was harvested in April, barley in May. The crop was cut with sickles, and the grain beaten out by using a flail, the sharp hooves of the oxen, or a threshing-sled. The threshed grain was tossed in the air and the wind blew away the chaff.

Beans, lentils, fruit and vegetables were staple foods. Olives were pressed for oil used for cooking and to fuel lamps. Figs and grapes were dried—and the grapes were also made into wine. Sheep, goats and cows provided milk and cheese.

The olive harvest

Preparing the ground for sowing

Sep
Oct
Nov
Dec
Jan
Feb

Picking and pressing the grapes

Reaping and threshing

Sept
Aug
July
June
May
April

CHAPTER 7

Critics of Jesus

Matthew felt a new person now that he had met Jesus. He wanted all his friends to meet Jesus too, so he decided to invite them all to a celebration party, where Jesus would be the most important guest.

Everyone had a wonderful time. And as they listened to Jesus talking, Matthew's friends discovered that God loved them and was ready to forgive them, however much other people might criticize and despise them.

But some of the religious leaders found out what kind of party Jesus was at, and began to cross-question his disciples.

'If your master is supposed to be such a good man, how can he mix with riff-raff like that?' they asked. 'It's bad enough when we come across tax collectors and sinners by accident and can't avoid them. But he's chosen to go to dinner with them. Your master is no better than they are.'

The disciples were indignant but didn't know how to reply. Jesus overheard, and answered these Pharisees himself.

'Who does the doctor visit?' he asked them. 'Those who are well or those who are sick? Fit people don't need a doctor. Respectable people don't look for my help, either, so I've come to search for those who know they are sinners. People who are ready to admit that they've gone wrong, who know they need me, find forgiveness and help.'

The Pharisees looked at Jesus in silence. Did he really think that they were too good to need God's help?

Then Jesus added, 'Don't forget the Scripture that says God would rather see people being kind than sticking strictly to religious rules.'

'Stick to the rules!'

Rules, rules, rules! Hundreds of extra regulations had been added over the years to the law that God gave the nation through Moses. Many religious people, like the Pharisees, who did not need to work hard for a living, spent all their time trying to keep every tiny law.

'If Jesus is a good man, why doesn't he do the same?' they wondered. But instead of criticizing Jesus, they picked on his disciples.

'Why don't your disciples wash their hands in the right way before they eat?' they asked him.

Jesus answered by asking them a question. 'Why do you take no notice of God's laws and follow your own rules instead? You don't obey God's command to care for your parents; you get round it by saying that your money is set aside for God and can't be used to help the family. Isaiah's words, spoken long ago, fit you exactly. He said, "These people teach man-made rules as though they were God's laws! Their worship means nothing to me, because they don't put their religion into practice."'

Inside and out

A crowd of people had heard what Jesus said to the Pharisees and had seen them turn away, mystified. Jesus explained a bit more:

'Listen everyone,' he said. 'Nothing that goes into a person from the outside can make him unclean. But what comes from inside does!'

The disciples were puzzled by these words and, later on, when the crowd had gone home, they asked Jesus, 'What did you mean about what goes in and what comes out? We can't make head or tail of it.'

Jesus was disappointed.

'I don't believe you understand any better than the crowds do,' he said. 'Listen! The fact that you haven't washed your hands in a special way isn't going to make you unclean in God's eyes, nor is the kind of food you eat. The uncleanness God dislikes is already inside you, waiting to come out. I'm talking about things like temper and spite, greed and jealousy. Think of the horrible actions they lead to! That's what makes you unclean in God's eyes.'

The disciples were quiet for a moment. Then one of them remarked, 'Well, you upset those Pharisees by what you said.'

'You need not worry about them,' Jesus replied. 'God knows the ones whose faith in him is real. The rest of the leaders are like blind people trying to guide blind people. You know what happens next—they all end up in the ditch!'

God's special day

Wherever Jesus and his followers went, a crowd of people was listening and watching. Some were in trouble, and had come to ask Jesus for help. Others wanted to hear him explain the Good News of God's kingdom.

Some of the religious leaders and Pharisees—those who were fast becoming Jesus'enemies, stayed close to him too. They were still looking for

excuses to find fault with him or with his disciples.

One Sabbath day, Jesus and the Twelve cut across the fields on their way to synagogue. By God's law, passersby were allowed to pick and eat any ripe fruit or grain growing in the fields they reminded them. 'The Sabbath was made for us and for our good, we were not made to serve the Sabbath. And the Son of man is Lord of everything, including the Sabbath.'

The disciples were not sure what Jesus meant by that, but they knew by the way he taught God's laws that he had set them free.

When they arrived at the synagogue they saw a man waiting for them whose hand was so damaged he could not use it.

'Come up here to the front!' Jesus called out to him. The man got up and stood beside Jesus. Then Jesus looked at the tense, tight-lipped faces of his critics—all waiting to pounce on him if he broke the Sabbath by healing the man, for that would count as 'work'.

'What do you think the law allows us to do on the Sabbath?' Jesus asked them. 'Should it be a day for helping others or for hurting them? Should we save someone's life—or destroy it?'

Jesus saw the hard, cold stare of his critics and felt angry. They did not care about the man, whose useless hand meant that he could not earn a living or care for his family. They only wanted to catch Jesus out. At the same time he felt sorry for them. They were so blind and stubborn.

'Stretch out your hand!' he told the man. As soon as he tried to move his useless hand, he found that it was as strong and good as the other one.

The Pharisees slipped quietly away, without saying a word. But they began to make plans to kill Jesus.

walked through. So the hungry disciples picked the ripe ears of grain, to eat as they went along.

Some Pharisees who were walking close behind hurried to catch them up. 'Do you see how your disciples are breaking the Sabbath?' they asked Jesus. He understood what they meant. They were accusing the disciples of working on the Sabbath. They thought that picking ears of corn counted as harvesting; rubbing them to get rid of the chaff counted as threshing.

'God's law about no work on the Sabbath is meant for our benefit,' Jesus

The old and the new

'Why don't you do the same as the Pharisees?' some people asked Jesus. 'They go without food several times a week.'

Some of John the Baptist's followers joined in: 'John taught us to fast, too. Why don't you make your disciples do the same?'

'When did you go to a wedding and sit down at the table and eat—nothing?' Jesus asked.

Everyone laughed. 'Of course we all feast and celebrate at the wedding party, while the bridegroom is there. Once he goes, that will be time enough to fast.'

Some of the disciples remembered how John the Baptist had described Jesus as the bridegroom, and himself as the bridegroom's friend, glad to be in his company. The disciples were as happy as guests at a wedding, because they had Jesus with them.

'Old and new don't mix,' Jesus went on. 'If you have to mend a hole in your coat you patch it with old cloth. New material would shrink when you washed it and you'd be left with a bigger hole than ever.

'Newly-made wine must be stored in a new goatskin, to give it room to expand. New wine would burst an old, dry skin, and you'd lose the lot.

'My teaching is new. It won't fit into the old ways of thinking and doing. It's not surprising that some people prefer to cling to the old ways. No one who has been drinking old wine immediately likes the taste of new.'

The Right Way and the Wrong

'It is not the ones who say the right things, but those who do as my Father says who will enter my kingdom,' Jesus told his followers. He told these stories to explain what he meant.

THE STORY OF THE TWO BUILDERS

There was once a man who decided to build a house. He dug down deep, and built his foundation on rock.

When the wind blew and the rains came, torrents of water hit that house, but it stood firm, because it was soundly built. That builder is like the person who hears my words, and obeys them.

Another man built his house on sand, on the dried-up bed of a stream. The wind blew and the rain poured down and the water gushed beneath that house, and it fell with a mighty crash. The builder of that house is like the person who hears my words but does not put them into practice.

THE STORY OF THE TWO SONS

There was once a man who had two sons. One morning he said to the older one: 'Son, I'd like you to go and work in the vineyard today.'

'I don't want to,' he answered. But later on he changed his mind and went.

Then the father went to his other son and asked: 'Will you go and work in the vineyard today?'

'Yes, Father!' he replied. But he never went.

'Which son did as his father wanted?' Jesus asked the listening people.

'The older one,' they replied.'

'Yes,' Jesus agreed, 'and I'm telling you that even the tax collectors and prostitutes are going into the kingdom before you. They repented when they heard John the Baptist preach. They changed their ways and did what he said. But you refused to obey his preaching.'

THE STORY OF THE TWO MEN WHO PRAYED

There were once two men who went to the temple to pray. One was a Pharisee and the other a tax collector.

The Pharisee stood apart from those who might not be as good as he was, and prayed to himself like this:

'I thank you, God, that I am not greedy or dishonest like everybody else. I thank you that I am not like that tax collector over there. I fast twice every week and I give you a tenth part of all I earn.'

But the tax collector stood at a respectful distance and did not even dare to look up. He wrung his hands and hung his head, pleading, 'Please, God, have mercy on me, a sinner!'

'I tell you,' Jesus said, 'the tax collector, not the Pharisee, was the one who went home right in God's sight. God does not listen to the proud but he is ready to help the humble.'

CHAPTER 8

A New Way to Live

The disciples had listened to what Jesus had to tell the Pharisees about keeping all the rules.

'Are you saying that we need not keep Moses' law any longer?' they asked him.

'Certainly not!' Jesus answered. 'I haven't come to do away with God's laws but to show how they are really meant to be kept.'

As they talked, he led them to the top of a grassy hill, where they could sit down and listen while he explained things to them.

The law of love

'The laws God gave through Moses will never be out of date,' Jesus said. 'They will last as long as life goes on. But the endless rules and regulations that the Pharisees and law teachers have added do not help you to obey them.

'Listen! The law says that if you kill someone, you must be punished. But murder begins in the heart—when you are angry or jealous, or hate someone. If you are really going to keep God's law, you must deal with the bad feelings inside you, not just with the crime of murder. God's laws teach us to love him and to love one another, not simply to keep a set of rules. We must obey God from the heart.

'The rules say that you must not be unfaithful to your marriage partner and if you want a divorce you must sign the right papers. But God made marriage to last a lifetime. He wants couples to be loving and faithful to each other, without even looking longingly at someone else's partner.

'You have been told that as long as you love your friends, it's all right to hate your enemies. But the law of love says, "Be kind to your enemies too." You see,

if you are going to take after your Father in heaven, you must behave in the same way that he does. God sends sun and rain for everyone—good and bad alike! He gives his good gifts to those who don't deserve them, as well as those who do. You should be like God—loving and giving. It's the generous, open-handed people who will themselves receive happiness and love.

'Don't criticize others. Imagine someone with a big plank of wood stuck in his eye offering to remove a tiny speck from someone else's! No one is so free of faults that he can see straight enough to put others right.'

How to be really happy

'I'll tell you who the truly happy people are,' Jesus went on. 'They are the ones who recognize how poor they are in God's eyes.

'Happy people are those who are sorry for their own sins and failures and who share the sadness of all who suffer and mourn.

'The happy ones are the humble ones, not too proud to receive what God has to give them.

'The happy ones are those who long to do right and follow God's ways.

'The happy ones are those who are kind and caring to others.

'The happy ones are those whose wholehearted aim is to please and serve God.

'The happy ones are those who work to bring about peace in the family and in the world around.

'The happy ones are those who are badly treated because they are my followers. Be glad if people hate you and say all kinds of bad things about you because you belong to me. There's a

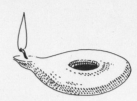

*'Ask God for what you need,' Jesus told his listeners,
'because he is your Father in heaven and loves to give
good things to his children.'*

THE STORY OF THE VISITOR AT MIDNIGHT

I magine that an unexpected visitor arrives on your doorstep in the middle of the night, tired and hungry! You have no food to give him, so you go to your friend's house and knock on his door.

'Please lend me three loaves!' you call out. 'A visitor has arrived and I've nothing to give him!'

From inside the house your friend shouts back, 'Don't disturb me! The door is locked and the children are fast asleep in bed. Go away!'

But you don't give up! You knock a bit harder and call a bit louder! In the end, he may not give you what you want because you are his friend, but he'll bring you the bread just to keep you quiet!

*'So keep asking God for what you need,' Jesus said.
'He isn't unwilling to hear, like that friend. He will
give you the best gift he has—his Holy Spirit.'*

THE STORY OF THE STONYHEARTED JUDGE

T here was once a hard-hearted judge, who cared for no one. A poor widow, who had been cheated out of her money, lived in the same town. Whenever the judge set foot outside his house, the widow would be there, waiting.

'Please hear me!' she would beg. 'Give me justice!'

For a long time the judge took no notice, but at last he said, 'I don't care about this woman or her rights, but I am so sick of her that I will settle her case.'

*'How much more will God, who is just and loving,
hear his people's cries for help?' Jesus ended.*

wonderful time coming for you in heaven!'

The disciples were dumbfounded. Everything Jesus said seemed upside down. His way of happiness was just the opposite of what everyone else believed.

'How should we pray?'

'Some of the religious people don't really talk to God when they pray,' Jesus said. 'They just make long speeches to impress anyone who may be watching them in the synagogue. When you pray, don't show off. Find a place on your own, then talk to your Father. Use simple words and mean what you say.'

'You are always praying,' the disciples said. 'Will you teach us how to do it?'

'Here is the pattern for prayer,' Jesus replied. 'Say this:

Our Father in heaven:
May your holy name be honoured;
may your kingdom come;
may your will be done on earth as it is
    in heaven.
Give us today the food we need.
Forgive us the wrongs we have done,
as we forgive the wrongs that others
    have done to us.
Do not bring us to hard testing,
but keep us safe from the Evil One.

'Don't ever forget the need to forgive others,' Jesus added. 'If you come to God refusing to forgive someone else, you cannot receive God's free forgiveness yourself.'

'How many times ought I to forgive someone who wrongs me?' Peter asked. 'As many as seven times?'

'Seventy times that!' Jesus answered. 'God forgives you times without number. You must do the same to others.'

'Stop worrying!'

'When you put God first, you can stop worrying,' Jesus told the disciples. 'Look at it this way. God is a loving Father: he will see that you have what you need. He feeds the birds—and they don't even lend a hand by sowing and getting in the harvest.'

Jesus stooped and gently touched one of the jewel-bright anemones growing wild at their feet.

'Look at these flowers,' he said. 'They don't sew or make their own clothes: yet King Solomon, in all his glory, never looked as lovely as they do. God can take care of all your needs.

'Worry never helped anyone live a day longer or grow an inch taller. Just deal with today's problems as they come— and let tomorrow's problems wait for tomorrow to arrive.'

Salt and light

'You are like salt in the world,' Jesus told the disciples. They thought hard. Salt kept fish and meat from going bad. Salt made food tasty. They could guess what Jesus wanted them to be like.

'Imagine a batch of salt that has lost its saltiness!' Jesus went on. 'It's no good to anyone. There's no way of putting the saltiness back into it again. It's only fit to be thrown out. So see that you are salty salt!'

'You are light in the world, too,' Jesus said. 'When you light a lamp, you don't hide it away out of sight. You put it on the lampstand, as high up as you can, so that it provides light for everyone in the house.

'See that you let your light shine out for others. Let them see your good deeds: then they will give praise to God, your Father.'

The Kingdom of God

'How can I describe the kingdom of God? What story
will help to explain it?' Jesus often asked. Then he would
tell his listeners stories of everyday life, each one intended
to teach them something new about his kingdom.

THE STORY OF THE MUSTARD SEED

God's kingdom is like a mustard seed, tiny as it lies in the palm of your hand. But plant it in the ground and it grows so large that the birds can perch on its branches and rest in its shade.

THE STORY OF THE YEAST

When a mother bakes bread, she mixes a tiny amount of yeast with a large quantity of flour. But it's powerful enough to make the whole batch of dough rise. That's like the kingdom of God!

THE STORY OF THE SEED GROWING SECRETLY

The kingdom of God is like a farmer who has sown his seed. He carries on as usual, sleeping at night and working by day. All the while the seed is mysteriously growing. The farmer does not know how it happens. It has nothing to do with his efforts. He is just glad when harvest comes and he can reap his grain.

THE STORY OF THE WEEDS

One day a farmer sowed his field with good seed. But at night, when everyone was sound asleep, an enemy came secretly and sowed weeds among the grain. No one knew what had happened until the two kinds of plant sprouted.

'You sowed good seed, so why are there so many weeds in the field?' his farm workers asked.

'An enemy has played a trick on me,' he told them.

'Shall we pull up the weeds, then?' they asked. But the farmer shook his head.

'You might pull up good grain, too, by mistake,' he warned. 'Let the two crops grow together until harvest comes. Then we'll sort out the good from the bad!'

'What does that story mean?' the disciples asked Jesus.

'The field is the whole world,' Jesus explained, 'and the good seed is God's word—the message I have come to bring. But the Evil One has been busy sowing weeds. For the present, my true followers, and those who only *pretend* to be mine, live alongside one another in my kingdom. But Harvest Day is coming. Then my angels will separate the true people from those who are false. The wrongdoers will be thrown out. But my people will shine like the sun in their Father's kingdom!'

THE STORY OF THE DRAGNET

The kingdom of God is like a fisherman's net. All kinds of fish swim into it. When the net is full, the fishermen bring it on shore, and sort out the fish. The good fish are put in the bucket and kept but the worthless ones are thrown out. At the end of the age, my angels will sort out the good from the bad in my kingdom.

THE STORY OF THE HIDDEN TREASURE

There was once a man who, quite by accident, found a treasure hoard, buried in a field. He covered it over quickly and went off, bursting with excitement. He determined to buy that field, whatever it cost: then the treasure would be his by right.

He had to sell everything he owned to buy it, but he did not mind. He had found something worth more than everything else he possessed. That's like the person who discovers God's kingdom.

THE STORY OF THE COSTLY PEARL

There was once a merchant who found a rare and beautiful pearl for sale. He set his heart on owning it.

It cost so much that he had to sell everything else he owned in order to buy it. But he willingly did so, just to own that one, perfect pearl of great value. That's like the kingdom of God.

Every Jewish boy learned a craft. The father usually taught his son his own trade and passed on his tools. Carpenters were well-respected, but the smell of a copper smelter, tanner or dung collector was considered grounds for divorce! Craftsmen wore a badge of office: a bone needle for a tailor, or a bright bit of cloth for a dyer. In Jesus' day there was plenty of work for stone-cutters, masons and woodworkers on one of King Herod's great building projects.

The picture shows builders at work on a house, the carpenter's workshop and a busy potter. All these were essential everyday crafts: so too were spinning and weaving and leatherwork.

The People Who Matter

One day, so many people tried to push their way into Peter's house, to see Jesus, that the disciples could scarcely keep them all in order.

'There's no time to stop for dinner!' one of them murmured to another. And a few hours later, 'No time for supper either!'

Jesus worked on, talking and healing. He never seemed hurried or flustered. He gave each person his full attention. However ill or anxious they were when they arrived, Jesus met their need. They loved him very much.

But when Jesus' family heard how hard he was working, they decided they should talk some sense into him. 'He must be off his head!' they said.

When they arrived, they could not get near to Jesus because of the crowd. But the news soon spread.

'Your mother and the family are outside and they want to see you,' someone told Jesus.

Jesus looked at the eager faces turned towards him: 'Who is my mother? Who are my brothers?' he asked.

There was a puzzled silence. Surely everyone knew the answer! But Jesus pointed first to one and then to another of his surprised disciples. 'Look!' he said. 'These are the members of my family. The person who does what God wants is my mother, my brother and my sister.'

A message from prison

Day after day, John the Baptist lay in the dark depths of Herod's dungeon. His strong, active body was held fast by chains, but his mind still twisted and turned.

Had he been wrong to warn his hearers in the desert of fire and wrath to come? He had been so certain that the Messiah would execute God's judgment on the wicked. Now his followers kept telling him about all Jesus' acts of healing and love. Had John made a terrible mistake? Perhaps Jesus was not the powerful, God-sent Messiah after all.

At last he could bear the pain and uncertainty no longer. He sent some of his followers to question Jesus. When they arrived, Jesus was busy healing many people. Some were blind and he gave them back their sight. Others were full of guilt and he forgave them, or tormented by evil spirits and he set them free.

'John sent us to ask if you really are the Messiah, or if we must look for someone else,' they said.

'Go back and tell John all the things that you have seen,' Jesus told them. 'The blind have their sight given back to them, the deaf hear again, and the poor learn about God's Good News. Happy is the one who has no doubts about me!'

Jesus knew that John would remember the words which the prophet Isaiah had written centuries before. He had described the servant Messiah, who would bring healing and good news to the sick and poor in Israel.

Then, as John's disciples went thoughtfully away, Jesus looked at the critical faces of the people in the crowd.

'What did you expect to find, when you went to the desert to hear John preach?' Jesus asked them. 'Not a courtier dressed in fine clothes! A prophet? Yes, the greatest prophet that has ever lived!

'But although our way of life and our preaching is so different, you have found fault with us both. You are just like the children who play games in the market-place. First they won't join in and play at funerals, then they won't play at weddings either. John lived a hard life, often fasting, and you accused him of being demon-possessed. I eat and drink like everyone else, and you accuse me of being a glutton and drunkard. But time will show who is wise in God's eyes.'

Children welcome!

One day, when the crowd around Jesus was as thick as ever, a group of women tried to push their way to the front. Some carried babies and others held small children tightly by the hand.

'We want Jesus to give our children his blessing,' they told the disciples, but the disciples shook their heads and stopped them getting closer.

'You mustn't bother the Master,' they told them. 'He's far too busy dealing with important people to spare time for children.'

Jesus saw what was happening and spoke sharply to the disciples. He said: 'Don't ever let me see you turning children away!'

Then he called to the children, who darted between the legs of the grown-ups to reach Jesus. The mothers followed, more shyly, and handed their babies to Jesus to hold. He took each one in turn, laid his hands on every child, and gave each one his blessing.

'God's kingdom belongs to children like these,' he told the disciples. 'No one can come into my kingdom unless they

guest. He did not greet him with a kiss, as the custom was, or send for a servant to wash his dusty feet and refresh his head with a little oil.

As they ate their meal in the cool courtyard, with its gently splashing fountain, a woman came in, crying softly

become as trusting and obedient as these children.'

An invitation out

Jesus was asked out to dinner by a Pharisee called Simon. In spite of his beautiful home and many servants, Simon did not treat Jesus like a special as she made her way around the table to Jesus.

She stooped beside him, her tears falling on his dusty feet. Gently, she wiped them dry with her long hair. Then she brought out an alabaster flask, broke the seal, and poured the precious perfume over his feet.

Simon looked across in disgust. He knew perfectly well who she was—a really bad woman from down town. If Jesus was a prophet from God, he thought, he would not let a woman like that come anywhere near him.

Jesus knew what he was thinking. 'Simon,' he said, 'I have something to say to you.'

'I'm listening,' Simon replied.

'There were once two men who owed money to a money-lender. One owed five hundred silver coins and the other owed five. Neither of them could pay him back, so—he let them both off their debt!'

Simon smiled a little at the joke. Whoever heard of a money-lender like that?

Then Jesus went on: 'Which of those two debtors will love the money-lender more?'

'I suppose the one who owed him most money,' Simon replied, in an offhand way.

'Absolutely right!' Jesus agreed. He looked at the woman, then said to Simon. 'Do you see what she has done for me? The very things you failed to do for your guest. She has shown me all this love because she realizes how much she has been forgiven.'

Then Jesus said to her, 'Your sins are forgiven.'

A look of peace and happiness spread over the woman's face.

But the guests at table said to one another, 'Who does he think he is, forgiving people's sins?'

THE STORY OF
The Unforgiving Servant

*Jesus told this story to explain why we should always
forgive other people.*

There was once a king who decided it was time for his servants to
settle the debts they owed him. While he was checking his
accounts, one of his servants was brought to him, who owed the king a
huge amount of money. He would have had to be a millionaire to pay
him back.

'If you can't pay me in money,' the king said, 'you had better be sold
as a slave, along with your wife and children. That will help to pay off
your debt.'

But the servant fell on his knees, begging for mercy.

'Just give me time,' he pleaded, 'and I will pay it all back.'

The king knew that was impossible and he felt sorry for him. 'I'll
forgive you your debt,' he said kindly. 'You can go free.'

With a huge sigh of relief, the servant left the king's presence. Outside
the throne room he caught sight of one of the other servants who owed
him a very small sum. He grabbed hold of him, insisting that he should
pay him back at once.

The second servant pleaded, 'Please give me time and I will give you
the money.'

'I shall do nothing of the kind!' the first servant shouted angrily. He
threw the second servant into prison until he could pay his debt.

The rest of the servants were furious and told the king about it. He
sent for the first servant.

'You wicked, worthless servant!' he said. 'I forgave you the huge
amount you owed me. How could you treat your fellow-servant as you
did? You are the one who will be punished in prison!'

*Jesus added, 'That is how my Father in heaven will
treat you, if you don't forgive others from your heart
when they hurt or wrong you.'*

CHAPTER 10

Who Can He Be?

Evening had come, and still the crowds lingered by the lake, not wanting to miss one story that Jesus might tell. He had been sitting in Peter's boat, close to the shore, so that everyone could see and hear him, as he told them the good news of God's kingdom.

At last Jesus signalled to his friends to join him in the boat.

'Let's cross to the other side of the lake,' he said.

The fishermen among them took the oars, while Jesus moved to the back of the boat. He was very tired and the rocking of the waves made him drowsy. He knew that he could trust his friends to handle the boat, so he lay down, with a cushion behind his head, and in no time was fast asleep.

But the gentle movement of the water grew stronger. A fierce wind, funnelling down from the hills on to the low-lying lake, began to whip the ripples into swelling waves. The disciples tried, with all their strength and skill, to keep the boat on course, but soon huge waves were breaking over the side and the boat was filling with water more quickly than they could bail it out.

Jesus slept peacefully on, until at last the frightened and desperate disciples staggered to the back of the boat. One of them shook him by the shoulders.

'Wake up!' they shouted above the noise of the wind. 'We're all going to be drowned. Don't you care?'

Jesus opened his eyes, got to his feet and looked at the turbulent water.

'Be still!' he ordered the wind. Then he said to the waves, 'Be quiet!'

Like a dog obeying its master's orders, the wind sank to a whisper and was still. The roaring subsided and the waves became quiet.

'Why were you frightened?' Jesus asked his friends. 'Didn't you trust me to keep you safe?'

They looked at each other, ashamed. But they were baffled too. As they took up the oars again, they asked each other, 'Who can he really be? Even the wind and the waves obey him.'

Wild man among the rocks

The boat reached the far shore and as they stepped on to dry land they could make out the figure of a man, looming up in the half-light of evening. Their hearts lurched as they recognized the wild man of the tombs. Terrible tales were told of his incredible strength. The people from his town tried time and again to chain him up, but he broke free and roamed the cave tombs, half naked, making the rocks echo to his bloodcurdling cries.

Now he had caught sight of Jesus and was pounding towards him, shrieking out, 'Jesus, son of God Most High, what are you going to do to me?'

The disciples shrank back, huddled together, but Jesus stepped forward and asked him, in a clear voice, 'What is your name?'

'My name is Legion,' the man wailed. 'A whole army of demons possesses me.'

Then they heard the mean, whining tones of the tormenting spirits: 'Don't send us far away,' the demons wheedled. 'Let us go into that herd of pigs.'

'Very well,' Jesus agreed. 'I give you permission.'

Next moment, the whole herd of pigs, which had been rooting peacefully on the side of the hill, began to squeal and panic. All of a sudden they rushed helter-skelter down the steep hillside, into the waters of the lake.

The man himself watched them, then sighed a deep sigh of contentment. Now he was certain that the evil spirits which had plagued him for so long were gone for ever: drowned. He sat quite still, looking up with love and wonder into Jesus' face.

Soon the people from his town came running, to see with their own eyes what had really happened. There was the madman they so much feared, properly dressed and sitting quietly, listening with understanding to what Jesus was saying. But they were not pleased.

'You'd better clear out of here,' they told Jesus. 'We don't want your sort, interfering with our lives.'

Jesus did not argue with them. He turned back to the boat, followed by the disciples.

The man who had been Legion rushed forward too. 'Please let me come with you!' he begged Jesus.

But Jesus gently shook his head. He had other work for him to do. This man was free to go where Jesus had been turned away.

'Go to your own home town,' he said, 'and tell them how much God has done for you.'

The Very Important Person

As soon as the boat was spotted returning across the lake, a crowd began to collect on the shore. They jostled and pushed to get close to Jesus as he stepped off the boat.

But they stood aside for one particular person, who made his way urgently to Jesus. They had recognized Jairus, a very important person in the town and a

leader of the synagogue.

With no thought of his own importance—or his fine clothes—Jairus fell to his knees on the hard stones.

'Please come with me!' he begged Jesus. 'My little daughter is dying. If you put your hands on her I believe she will get better.'

Jesus gently pulled him to his feet and they set off, as quickly as the crowds would let them, towards Jairus' home.

The woman in the crowd

No one noticed the thin, pale woman, who squeezed past the burly backs of the men to get close to Jesus. Hurrying alongside him, she stretched out her hand and clutched quickly at the edge of his tunic. In another moment she had let it go and disappeared again into the crowd.

But Jesus stood still, looking around at the heaving, surging mass of people. When Jairus tugged anxiously at his sleeve, he still did not move.

'Who touched me?' he asked in a clear voice.

The disciples laughed. 'What a question to ask!' one of them said. 'Just look—everyone is bumping into you and touching you!'

'But someone touched me in a different way,' Jesus explained, 'someone who wanted to be healed.'

Then the woman came forward, out of the crowd. She was trembling all over as she knelt at Jesus' feet.

'I was the person who touched you,' she admitted. 'For twelve long years I have been ill with bleeding that would not stop. I've spent all my money on doctors and they have made me worse rather than better. I was certain that if I could even touch your tunic I would be cured. And the moment I did so the

bleeding stopped and I knew that I was healed.'

Jesus looked at her with kindness. He knew how much she had suffered. By Jewish law, her illness had kept her from mixing with others and going to synagogue. Now she was fit and free to enjoy life again.

'Go in peace,' he said, 'your faith has made you well.'

'Get up, little one!'

Jairus was beside himself with worry at the delay. When he saw some of his own servants hurrying towards him, his heart sank.

'There is no point in troubling Jesus now,' one of them said. 'Your little daughter has died.'

Jairus hid his face in his hands, overcome with sadness and despair.

Then he felt Jesus' strong hand on his shoulder.

'Don't be afraid, Jairus,' Jesus said. 'Just go on believing!'

Then, telling Peter and James and John to follow, he led Jairus firmly along the narrow street to his house. Already the mourning women were there, playing their flutes and wailing their sad dirges for the dead. Jesus signalled to them to stop as he strode through the archway and into the courtyard.

'There is no need for all this noise and lamenting,' he told them. 'The little girl is only asleep.'

They laughed out loud at such an absurd notion, but Jesus took no notice. Taking with him only the girl's parents and his three followers, he went into the room where the body lay.

He looked down at the still white form, then took her cold hand in his warm one and said, 'Time to get up, little one!'

The still body stirred, and the dark brown eyes opened wide. She looked at Jesus and smiled. The next moment she was out of bed and bounding across the room to her mother, full of life and health.

Jesus looked at her parents, who were shaking and crying with shock and joy.

'She's hungry,' he reminded them. 'Why don't you get her something to eat?'

Then he gave them strict orders not to tell anyone else what had happened that day.

Lake Galilee, deep below sea level, is surrounded by hills. Winds often funnel down, causing sudden violent storms. The lake was rich in fish at the time of Jesus, and many people earned their living fishing, or salting fish for export. The fishermen took their boats out at night, but they could also use a circular cast-net or a dragnet close to the shore. By day there were nets to mend and clean, after the catch was sorted and sold—or sent to the lake town of Magdala for salting.

A fishing-boat from the time of Jesus, recently discovered in the mud, is twenty-seven feet long and seven feet wide. It has a shallow draught and is pointed at both ends.

CHAPTER 11

Get Ready for the King!

Jesus wanted as many people as possible to hear the Good News of God's kingdom, so he planned to send the disciples out in different directions to teach and heal.

The disciples must have felt nervous. It was one thing to be Jesus' helpers, but quite another to go out on their own.

'Don't worry!' Jesus said, when he saw their doubtful looks. 'You will go in pairs, each with a friend. And I am going to give you my power so that you will be able to heal and drive out evil spirits.' Then he gave them his instructions.

'Travel light,' he told them. 'Don't be weighed down with extra clothes or food or money. Just take a stout stick to help you up hill and down. When someone offers you bed and breakfast, stay with them gladly. But if the people in any town refuse to listen to you, leave them to their own devices and go on to the next place.'

Full of a sense of adventure, the disciples set off. Everywhere they went they told those who would listen that the time had come to turn back to God, because Jesus, his King, had arrived. They healed those whose bodies were sick as well as those tormented by evil spirits. So the good news about Jesus spread far and wide.

Death of a hero

Rumours about Jesus had reached the palace of King Herod. He was disturbed and confused. The things he heard about Jesus reminded him of John the Baptist.

When Herod had shut John up in his grim desert fortress, he had not meant to harm him. Although John's blunt words made Herod feel guilty and uncomfortable, he still felt compelled to listen to his preaching. John's honest goodness showed up the fawning flatterers at court in their true light.

Herod's wife, Herodias, had no such mixed feelings. She hated John for telling them that they had done wrong. She was waiting her chance to get rid of this troublesome prophet once and for all.

On Herod's birthday he gave a splendid party. There were extravagant dishes of every kind, and wine ran freely among the invited men.

When all the guests were merry, the daughter of Herodias entertained them by dancing. The drunken guests loved it. There were clapping and catcalls when she ended her performance by bowing low before Herod's royal throne. He was as delighted as his guests.

'Ask me for anything you like,' he offered extravagantly, 'and I promise to give it to you.'

Her mind full of fine clothes and jewels, or even a palace of her own, she ran to ask her mother's advice.

'What shall I ask for?' she inquired.

With gleaming eyes Herodias answered: 'The head of John the Baptist on a dish.'

When Herod heard the strange and grisly request he was deeply sorry. He was frightened at the thought of executing someone as just and good as John, but he was even more afraid to lose face by going back on the promise that he had made in front of all his guests. So he gave orders for a guard to be sent to the dungeon, to cut off John's head and bring it to the girl. She took it to her mother.

John's faithful disciples were allowed to bury his body with proper reverence and with bitter tears.

Now Herod was frightened. Was this Jesus none other than John, come back to life?

Time to relax?

When Jesus heard the news of John's death he was very sad. John was part of the family and they had known and loved each other since they were boys. Jesus understood, too, how lonely and tough John's mission for God had been and how bitter the dark imprisonment in Herod's gloomy dungeon.

But soon the excited disciples were arriving back. They could not wait to tell

83

Jesus about everything that had happened to them on their preaching tour.

Jesus realized that, in spite of their enthusiasm, they were tired out. And there were still so many people coming and going that they couldn't even snatch time for a meal.

'Let's get right away on our own for a while,' Jesus said, 'and you can have some rest.'

So they set off in the boat out of Herod's domain, to the other side of the lake, where there were only the hills for company.

But the crowd got wind of their plans and, while the boat was making its way across the lake, more and more people began to run around the shore, to get there first.

Jesus and his friends pushed the boat on to the shingle, only to be greeted, once again, by a demanding crowd.

The disciples' hearts sank. But Jesus did not think of the people as a nuisance. Even his sadness about John was swallowed up by his loving care for every one of them. They seemed to him like lost, frightened sheep, with no shepherd to guide or protect them. He began at once to heal those who were ill and to tell them all the good news of God's love and forgiveness.

The biggest picnic

The time flew by and no one seemed to notice—no one except the disciples. As the sun began to go down they grumbled together for a while, then marched up to Jesus.

'Do send the people away!' they begged. 'It's getting late and if they don't hurry they won't be in time to get themselves food.'

'Then why don't *you* give them some?' Jesus said.

The disciples looked at one another despairingly. Was the Master joking?

They never knew what he would say next.

'We'd need a fortune to buy enough bread just to give everyone a mouthful,' Philip protested.

'Go and see if anyone here has brought food,' Jesus suggested. He knew already how he was going to solve the problem, but he wanted to encourage and help the disciples to trust him.

Andrew said eagerly, 'There's a lad here who has five rolls and two small fish.' Then he saw the amused smirks on the other disciples' faces and quickly added, 'But that won't go far.'

'Just get the people sitting down in groups of fifty,' Jesus told the disciples. It was springtime and the hill was covered with grass.

They did as Jesus said and at last the vast crowd of over five thousand was settled into some kind of order.

Then Jesus took the lad's bread and fish in his hands and gave thanks to God for it. He gave some to each of the disciples, who went from one group to the next, sharing out the bread and fish. However much they gave out, Jesus still had enough to refill their baskets.

When no one could manage another crumb, Jesus told the disciples not to waste the food that they had not yet shared. All twelve still had a full basket of bread and fish to keep for the next day's meals.

'It's a ghost!'

The picnic was over and night was falling.

'You go back across the lake,' Jesus told his disciples.

When the fishing-boat drew away from the shore, Jesus sent the crowds home. Then he climbed slowly up the hill, alone at last in the darkness.

But Jesus knew that he was not alone. God, his Father, was always with him, and Jesus longed for a chance to talk and listen to him in quietness. He often spent the nights this way: it was the only time when he was free from the crowds. For some hours he was aware only of his Father's closeness.

The wind had got up and although the disciples were rowing with all their strength they could make no headway. It was almost dawn and they were still only half-way across the lake. They felt exhausted and disheartened.

But Jesus hadn't forgotten them. He saw the tiny dot of a boat, struggling against the winds and currents, and came hurrying to help them, walking out to them on the waves.

When they caught sight of him, they were terrified.

'Look!' they shrieked. 'It must be a ghost!'

But Jesus' familiar voice rang out across the water.

'Don't be frightened!' he called out. 'It's me!'

Then, with a deep sigh of relief, the disciples squeezed up and made room for Jesus on board. At once the wind died down and their oars glided easily through calm water.

Who could their Master be, they wondered, to do such amazing things?

But one of them, at least, had guessed the secret. 'You are the Son of God!' he whispered in wonder.

Bread for life

People flocked around Jesus more than ever. They were looking for a Messiah and leader who would go on providing them with free meals, and Jesus knew it.

'You are following me because you ate the bread and fish,' he told them. 'But you don't understand the meaning behind that picnic. I myself am the bread that God has sent to satisfy your deepest needs. I am the bread of life. Put your trust in me and I will feed you so that you will live for ever.'

Who Am I?

Jesus and his disciples were in Bethsaida, a fishing town beside the lake, when a little group came up, leading a man by the hand.

'Please help our friend!' they pleaded. 'He wants to be able to see!'

Jesus looked at the anxious faces of the friends, and at the blank, sightless eyes of the man in front of him. He took him by the hand and led him out of the village away from the inquisitive stares of the crowd. There would be no frightening mass of faces here to confuse him when he could first see again.

Jesus moistened the man's sightless eyes with saliva, as a healer was expected to do. Then he put his hands reassuringly on the man's shoulders and asked, 'Can you see anything?'

The blind man peered around at the men and women coming towards them, anxious to catch up with Jesus.

'Yes,' he said doubtfully. 'I can see people, but they look more like walking trees!'

Again Jesus put his hands on the man's eyes.

This time the man looked hard and long, and a slow smile dawned on his face.

'I can see everything perfectly!' he said in wonder.

'Don't go back into the crowded town,' Jesus told him. 'Go straight home to your family.'

'You are God's King!'

Jesus and his friends left the lake and began the steep climb northwards to the villages that lay on the boundary of Israel, where the River Jordan has its source. As they walked they talked.

'Who do people think that I am?' Jesus asked them.

'Herod isn't the only one to think you are John the Baptist come back to life,' one of them answered. 'Plenty of others say so too.'

'Some think you are the prophet Elijah returned to earth, as God promised,' another said.

'Or one of the other great prophets,' someone else added. There was a little pause, as each thought of the things he had heard from the crowd.

Then Jesus stopped and scanned their faces.

'Who do *you* think I am?' he asked point blank.

'You are the Messiah!' Peter exclaimed fervently.

In an instant, all his previous doubts were gone. He was certain now who the Master was.

Jesus looked at the others and knew that Peter had been their spokesman. They believed as he did. Jesus was glad that God had made the secret known to them and that they accepted him as the long-promised King. But they must keep it a secret still. Most people were looking for a Messiah who would set up his throne in Jerusalem and organize a rebellion against Rome. Jesus was not going to be that kind of king. So he told them strictly: 'Don't tell anyone else who I am.'

The disciples were bubbling over with the excitement of discovering that Jesus was God's promised Messiah. They began to picture the day that must surely be coming, when Jesus would go to Jerusalem to be crowned. They would be his chief ministers!

Jesus' voice broke in on their daydreams. 'I must go to Jerusalem,' he said, 'where I shall be rejected and ill-treated by the leaders of the people. I shall be put to death—but three days later I will be raised to life again.'

The disciples were shocked and upset. How could Jesus say such dreadful things?

'Don't talk like that, Lord!' Peter exclaimed. 'You must not let that happen to you!'

Jesus turned to him and said, 'Peter, you are speaking with Satan's voice, trying to tempt me away from God's chosen path.'

There was a shocked silence. Then Jesus went on: 'Listen, if you want to be my disciples, you must take the road that

I am taking. Don't aim for power or wealth or success. Every follower of mine must forget self, take up the cross, like a criminal going to the gallows, and be prepared to lose everything for my sake.'

The disciples could not understand. They knew now that Jesus was the Messiah. Surely that meant that the future was bright and rosy, for him and for his followers. But, once again, the your true life. But cheer up! You will discover that the ones who are willing to lose everything for my sake are the very people who will, in the end, gain everything.

'There is a day coming when I shall return to earth in glory, with the holy angels. If you are not ashamed of me and my teaching, I shall make it known, far and wide, on that victory day, that you belong to me.'

The King in splendour

One evening, about a week later, when the disciples were still reeling from the new things that Jesus had been teaching them, he said:

'Peter, I want you and James and John to come with me up the mountain, where we can be on our own to pray.'

They climbed to the beautiful, swelling summit of a high mountain. But the three friends were tired and, while Jesus prayed, they fell fast asleep.

They awoke with a start, knowing something strange had happened. A glow lit up the evening sky. They looked at Jesus and saw that his face was shining and his clothes were a luminous, dazzling white. They could not take their eyes off their transformed, glorious Master. And as they looked, two other men appeared out of the darkness and

Master had shattered their ideas. He had given them a new puzzle to solve.

Jesus looked at their bewildered faces.

'Listen,' he said gently, 'the whole world is not worth winning if it costs you began talking to Jesus. Without being told, they knew them to be Moses, great leader and lawgiver of Israel, and Elijah, the mighty prophet, who had called Israel back from idol-worship to serve the true God. Both spoke to the Master as if he were *their* Master too.

The disciples listened to the conversation. They were not talking about Jesus' coronation, but about the death that he would die, in order to carry out God's great plan for humankind.

Bursting with nervousness and excitement, Peter exclaimed: 'Lord, this is wonderful! We'll make three tents— one for you, one for Moses and one for Elijah. Then we can stay here for ever!' He didn't know what he was saying.

At that moment a bright golden cloud came over them, hiding everything else from view. They knew it was the cloud of God's presence when they heard God's voice saying, 'This is my own dear Son, the one I have chosen. Listen to him!'

Instinctively, the awed and terrified disciples threw themselves face down on the rough ground. Then each, in turn, felt the gentle, strong hand of Jesus on his shoulder.

'Get up!' he said. 'And don't be frightened!'

Cautiously they opened their eyes and peered around. The vision had disappeared. Only their dear, familiar Master was standing close to them, looking his usual self.

As they retraced their steps down the mountain next morning, Jesus said, 'Don't tell anyone what you have seen— not until I have been raised from death.'

They wondered what Jesus meant by that. Then they asked him to answer another puzzling question: 'What do the teachers of the law mean when they say that Elijah will come back to earth before Messiah comes?'

' "Elijah" has come already,' Jesus told them, 'and they treated him badly, just as they will ill-treat me.'

Then it dawned on them that the promised Elijah was none other than John the Baptist, the one who had preached repentance and pointed the way to Jesus.

Down to earth again

They did not have long to think about all they had seen and heard. As they came closer to the village, they heard the buzz of excited voices. A man came rushing across to Jesus.

'Teacher,' he cried, 'please help my only son! He suffers from terrible fits and often falls into the fire or into the water. I brought him to your disciples, but they could do nothing to help.'

Jesus looked across to his followers, who were deep in argument with some of the teachers of the law.

'Bring your son to me!' he said.

At that moment the boy had another severe fit, and fell to the ground, foaming at the mouth.

'How long has he suffered this way?' Jesus asked.

'Ever since he was a little lad,' his father answered. 'Please have pity and help us—if you can!'

'If *you* can!' Jesus retorted. 'Everything is possible for the person who has faith.'

'I do believe!' the father said quickly. 'But please help me to trust you more!'

Jesus saw that the crowd was pressing in on them, so, with a word of command, he ordered the illness to go. The lad gave a piercing scream, shuddered, then lay motionless.

'He's dead!' some of the onlookers exclaimed, as they looked at his still body. But Jesus took his hand and helped him to his feet. He was completely well.

'Why couldn't *we* heal him?' the unhappy disciples asked Jesus, when they had him on his own.

'Prayer is what makes that kind of healing possible,' Jesus replied.

THE STORY OF
The Unemployed Workers

*Jesus often reminded people that God's kingdom is for
those humble enough to accept God's kindness and love,
even though they don't deserve it. No one can bargain
with God or hope to earn a place in his kingdom.*

There was once a man who went to the market-place early one
morning, to hire workers for his vineyard. He agreed to pay them
the regular wage of one silver coin for the day's work.

At nine o'clock, at noon, and at three, he went to the market again and
hired more workers.

It was nearly five when he went for the last time. There were still
some men standing around.

'Why have you done nothing all day?' he asked.

'Because no one has hired us,' they said miserably.

'Then come and work in my vineyard,' he told them.

When evening came, the owner instructed his foreman to pay all the
workers, beginning with those hired last.

To their delight, the latecomers were given the full day's wage of a
silver coin.

The men who had worked all day expected to get more, when their
turn came. But every worker received the same.

'That's not fair!' the first workers grumbled. 'We ought to get extra.
We worked through the heat of the day, not like these lazy latecomers!'

'Listen, friends,' the owner told them, 'I have not cheated you. I have
paid you what we agreed. It is for me to decide how I use my money. Are
you jealous because I have been generous to the others?'

*'In God's reckoning, the first often end up last and
the last first,' Jesus said at the end of the story.*

CHAPTER 13

The Good Time Coming

One Sabbath day Jesus was invited to a meal with one of the leading Pharisees. All the other guests watched Jesus closely. They wondered what he was going to do or say next.

Just then, a very sick man, whose arms and legs were badly swollen, made his way through the group of guests and begged Jesus to heal him.

The murmur of voices stopped. Now there might be some excitement. Everyone knew that their host would not approve if Jesus healed on the Sabbath.

Jesus looked at them and asked, 'Does our law allow healing on the Sabbath, or not?'

In the silence that followed he gave his full attention to the sick man. He healed him and sent him away. Then he said, 'Suppose you had a son who fell into a well on the Sabbath? What would you do? Or let's say it was only one of your animals that had the accident. Wouldn't you rush to haul it out?'

No one answered a word, but they understood what he meant.

Then the guests began to make their way to the top of the table, to get the best seats, near their host.

Jesus watched them and then he said, 'When you are invited to a wedding, don't rush for the best seats, near the top of the table. You'll feel very foolish if your host has to ask you to move further down, because someone more important has arrived and must have your seat. How much better to choose a place at the bottom of the table! Then your host may invite you, in front of all the other guests, to move higher up to a better seat!

'Self-important people will be brought down in the world, while those who don't think too highly of themselves will be made great.'

Some of the guests at the top of the table went red in the face. Others looked angrily at Jesus. A few wise ones understood that he was not only talking about how to behave at a dinner party.

Then Jesus turned to the Pharisee who had invited him.

'I have some advice for you, too,' he said. 'When you plan a dinner party, don't just invite the family and your best friends, or the rich and important people you know. They will invite you back to their homes and you will be repaid for your kindness. Instead, invite all the people who can't ask you back—the poor, the blind, the disabled. God is the one who will reward you for that hospitality, on the day that is coming, when good people rise from death.'

Who is the greatest?

The disciples thought a good bit about that 'day that was coming'. They were certain, now they knew that Jesus was the Messiah, that soon he would be crowned King in Jerusalem. And they would be his right-hand men.

Once more, as they walked beside the pale waters of the lake, he told them: 'I, the Son of man, will be handed over to be killed. But three days later I will rise to life again.'

Still, as they straggled along behind him, they shared their usual daydreams about the coming kingdom. And they still argued about who would have first place in it.

When they arrived at Peter's house, they went inside, out of the winter rain.

'What were you so busy talking about on the way?' Jesus asked them.

No one answered a word. Jesus looked down at the child who had clambered on to his knee. He set him gently down in the middle of the room and, with his arm around the child, said to his disciples, 'Do you want to be great in God's coming kingdom? If so, you must learn to change and become like this child—not self-important or proud of your own achievements. The one who thinks least about himself is the greatest one in my kingdom.

'Whoever welcomes a child, like this one, is really welcoming me. And whoever welcomes me, welcomes my Father, who sent me.'

'We want the best places!'

James and his brother John were among the first of the Twelve who Jesus called to follow him. Their father ran a thriving fishing business and their devoted mother was a follower of Jesus too. She thought that her sons should have top places when Jesus was crowned King,

and told them to put in their claim straight away.

So, one day, when the others were out of earshot, they said to Jesus, 'There's something we'd like you to do for us.'

'What is it?' Jesus asked, looking from them to their mother.

'We'd like you to promise us the two most important positions in your kingdom, once you are crowned King,' they blurted out.

Jesus answered sadly, 'You don't know what you are asking for. Can you share the suffering that lies ahead for me?'

'Of course we can!' they answered cheerfully.

'Yes,' Jesus agreed, 'you *will* suffer for my sake. But as to who will be my chief ministers—that is not for me to decide. My Father is the one who makes that choice.'

When the other disciples found out what James and John had been saying, they were very angry. But Jesus knew that was because, deep down, they were ambitious and self-seeking too. Once again he tried to explain that, in his kingdom, the way people usually think is turned upside down.

'Political leaders make themselves strong and powerful, and keep everyone else firmly under control,' he told them. 'You must not behave like that. If you are ambitious and want to be someone great, then—wait on everyone else and look after their needs. I've shown you the way, for that is what I have done. I didn't come here to to be waited on, but to look after others and give my life to bring many people back to God.'

THE STORY OF
The Great Feast

*Religious Jews often pictured God's kingdom as a splendid
banquet, at which they would be the guests.*

*As they all sat enjoying the meal at the Pharisee's home,
someone remarked, 'How wonderful it will be for the guests
who are invited to God's feast in his coming kingdom!'*

Then Jesus told this story.

There was once a man who planned a splendid feast and invited a
great many people. When everything was ready, and the table was
laden with tasty dishes, he sent out his servants to tell the guests that it
was time to come. But they all began to make excuses.

'I've just bought a field,' the first one explained. 'I must go and see it,
so I can't come.'

'And I've bought five pairs of oxen,' the next one said. 'I must go and
try them out. My apologies!'

The third one told them, 'I've just got married, so I can't possibly
come.'

The crestfallen servants went back to their master with the news. He
was furious that the guests he had invited were refusing to come. He
told his servants, 'Hurry up, and go instead to the back streets and
alleyways. Tell all the beggars to come to my house and enjoy my feast.'

The servants did as he said and soon a procession of ragged, dirty,
hungry people crowded into the house, scarcely able to believe their
good fortune. But there was still room for more.

'Go now to the country lanes and the hedgerows,' the master said,
'and find the tramps and those who are on the road. Invite them too, so
that my house will be full. For not one of the people first invited will
taste my feast.'

The country in which Jesus lived lies at the eastern end of the Mediterranean Sea. It is a small country with a long coastline bordered by flat and fertile land. Behind this, rocky hills run from north to south like a backbone. This is sheep country. The hills are broken by a deep rift valley, hot and humid. The River Jordan rises in the mountains of Lebanon in the far north and runs through Lake Galilee, south beyond Jericho to the Dead Sea—so salt that no living creature can survive in its waters. This is the lowest point on earth.

Galilee is especially fertile and well watered: all kinds of fruit and vegetables, as well as grain crops grow there. In spring the hillsides blaze with wild flowers. In summer even the grass is brown and dry. In Jesus' day all kinds of wild animals roamed the hills—bears, leopards, jackals and hyenas.

Mediterranean Sea

COASTAL PLAIN

DESERT
(WILDERNESS)

Capernaum

Nazareth

Lake
Galilee

Samaria (Sebaste)

River Jordan

HILL
COUNTRY

Jerusalem

Jericho

Dead
Sea

CHAPTER 14

From North to South
–and Home Again

Jesus spent most of his time teaching and healing in the fishing towns of the north, around Lake Galilee. But, when the Jewish festivals drew near, he and his disciples, with hundreds of other pilgrims, made their way to Jerusalem, to worship and celebrate at the temple.

The city was always bursting at the seams. Everywhere there were families up from the country, enjoying the noise and smells and excitements of the great city.

Above all, their eyes were drawn to the temple itself, high up, glistening with white marble and glinting with gold, so beautiful it took the breath away. Sooner or later they would make their way up the broad, stone steps to the gates of the temple courts.

Once, when Jesus was in Jerusalem for a festival, he walked beside a pool, near the Sheep Market. As he picked his way along the columned porch, he could hear the grumbles and groans of the sick people, who were stretched out on the ground all around, or crouching miserably beside the pool. They were all waiting for the spring beneath the pool to bubble up, as it did from time to time. They believed that whoever was first into the pool when the water moved and swirled would be cured of their sickness.

Jesus stopped beside a man lying motionless.

'Do you want to get better?' he asked him. Jesus knew that he had been ill for thirty-eight years. As the man met Jesus' gaze, he realized that this stranger knew all about him and understood his deepest thoughts.

'It's not my fault I've been like this all these years,' he grumbled. 'I can't move an inch, and there's no one to help me into the water.'

'Get up!' Jesus told him. 'Pick up your sleeping-mat and walk!'

As if in a dream, the man did as Jesus told him. To his amazement, he could move and he could walk. Without another word, he set off into the city.

He had not gone far when he saw a group of the religious leaders coming towards him. One of them put up a warning hand.

'Stop!' he ordered. 'What do you think you are doing, carrying your sleeping-mat on the Sabbath? Don't you know that you are breaking the law?'

'It's not my fault,' the man insisted. 'I'm only doing what I was told to by the man who healed me.'

His accusers looked knowingly at one another.

'And who was that?' one of them

angrier. He had dared to say that God was his father and talked as if he was God's equal. They were more than ever determined to kill him.

Teacher in the temple

Jesus went back to Galilee. The threats of the religious Jews in Jerusalem made it too dangerous to stay in the south. He waited until the Festival of Shelters was half-way through before going back, secretly, to Jerusalem.

But there were eyes everywhere, combing the crowds to see if Jesus was among the pilgrims. The religious leaders wanted to find him so that they could have him arrested. The ordinary people wanted to listen to him or watch him perform miracles.

'Who do you think he is?' they whispered to each other, not wanting the priests or Pharisees to overhear.

'He must be a good man, that's certain,' some said. But others argued, 'He can't be good if all the religious people are against him. They *must* know best.'

When the festival was nearly over, Jesus, like the other rabbis, took his place in one of the columned porches around the temple courts, and began to teach his followers. The religious leaders were baffled that Jesus could teach as he did without a college training.

'I'm not passing on my own ideas,' Jesus explained. 'I am bringing you God's words. Everyone who is willing to obey God will know that what I am saying is true.'

On the very last day of that festival, an offering of water was poured out to God. It was drawn from the spring of Siloam, which provided water for the city.

In full view of the watching crowds,

asked sharply.

'I don't know!' the man answered. He looked back, craning his neck, but Jesus was nowhere to be seen.

Reluctantly, they let him go and he made his way to the temple court. There Jesus met him again.

'Listen,' Jesus said sternly, 'you are well again now. Stop sinning, or something worse may happen to you.'

No one but Jesus and the man himself knew why he warned him in that serious way.

The man went straight to find the Jewish leaders.

'I know now who healed me,' he told them. 'It was Jesus.'

They nodded. They had guessed as much. They must redouble their efforts to stop his teaching.

Soon they found Jesus themselves and accused him harshly of breaking the Sabbath. But Jesus replied: 'My Father never stops work, so I must go on working too. I must use all the time I have to heal and save.'

This made the Jewish leaders even

Jesus called out: 'If you are thirsty, come to me! Put your trust in me, and a never-failing spring of water will bubble up within you. It will satisfy your deepest needs and overflow to bring life and refreshment to others too!'

The light of the world
There were beggars everywhere, lining the narrow streets of Jerusalem. Many whined and complained, but one of them, who had no sight, was making the others smile with his jokes and comic remarks.

'Why should he have been born blind?' the disciples asked Jesus. 'Was it a punishment because his parents had done something bad? Or was it his own fault?'

'No one is to blame,' Jesus said. 'His blindness is not a punishment. But it will give God the chance to show his power and greatness.'

As Jesus talked, he bent down and mixed some of the dry dust to mud by spitting on it. He put this paste on the man's sightless eyes and said to him: 'Go and wash your face in Siloam.'

The disciples guided the man to the nearby pool. When he washed off the mud-packs he found that he could see for the first time in his life.

An excited crowd soon clustered around him. Some prodded him to make sure he was real and peered at his face to see if he was the man they had known for so long.

'It's him all right,' the people who lived next door to him decided.

'No it isn't!' another friend insisted. 'It's his double.'

The man himself spoke up. 'It *is* me!' he said. '*I* ought to know!'

'Tell us what happened!' they all asked.

'The man called Jesus made some mud, rubbed it on my eyes, and then told me to wash in Siloam. The moment I did, I could see.'

They hustled him off to the Pharisees and made him tell *them* his story. The religious leaders listened keenly, carefully noting the fact that Jesus had

healed him on the Sabbath day. They cross-questioned the man again and again, until he was sick of it.

'I think you must want to be his followers too,' he teased, 'you want to know so much about Jesus.'

'How dare you!' they exclaimed. 'You may be his follower but we follow Moses. This Jesus is a sinner. He must be, if he healed you on the Sabbath.'

'I don't think a sinner would do a wonderful thing like giving me back my sight!' the man objected. 'I believe he has come to us from God.'

At this they threw him out of the synagogue, telling him never to come back.

But Jesus found him. He asked him, 'Do you believe in the Son of man and put your trust in him?'

'Who is he, Lord?' the man asked.

'You have met him already and he is the one talking to you now!' Jesus told him.

The man fell on his knees in front of Jesus. 'I *do* believe!' he said.

'I have come so that the blind should see and those who see should become blind,' Jesus said.

Some Pharisees were listening. 'Are you saying that we are blind and don't know the truth about God?' they asked.

'If you were blind,' Jesus told them, 'you would not be able to see the truth. But you are guilty because you claim to see and understand about God.

'I am the light of the world. Everyone who follows me will never walk in darkness but will have the light of life.'

The man who had been blind understood what Jesus meant. It was not only his eyesight that Jesus had given to him. Now he had eyes to understand and believe who Jesus really was. And that light had brought him freedom and new life.

The Kind Stranger

'What must I do to have eternal life?' a teacher law of the Jewish law asked Jesus. He hoped to catch him out.

'What do you think?' Jesus asked him. 'You are the one who studies the law.'

'Love God with all my heart and love the people around me as I love myself,' he replied.

'You are right,' Jesus said. 'That is the way to life.'

'But who are the people I should love?' the teacher persisted. He wanted to put himself in a good light. For answer, Jesus told him this story . . .

One day a man took the road from Jerusalem down to Jericho. Suddenly, robbers burst out from behind the high rocks, attacked him, stripped him, beat him up, then fled. There he lay, half dead, as the sun beat down.

After a while, a priest came by. But when he saw the wounded man he hurried past, on the other side of the road. A little later, a Levite came along, took a good look at the still body, then went quickly on.

At last a Samaritan came along. When he saw the poor victim he felt full of pity. He knelt beside him, cleaned his wounds with oil and wine and bandaged him up. Then he sat him on his own donkey and, gently supporting him, made his way to the nearest inn, where he looked after him.

Next day he asked the innkeeper to take care of the man until he was well enough to leave.

'Here are two silver coins for your trouble,' he said. 'If you spend more, I'll pay next time I pass.'

Then Jesus asked the law teacher, 'Which of those three treated the wounded man as someone to be loved?'

'I suppose it was the man who took care of him,' the teacher replied grudgingly.

'You go and behave in the same way,' Jesus said.

The good shepherd

Jesus saw that the religious leaders, who were concerned about keeping their list of rules, did not look after the people in their charge as God meant them to.

Hundreds of years before, the prophet Ezekiel had compared the leaders of the people to bad shepherds, neglecting their flock. Many of the Pharisees of Jesus' time were no better.

'I am the good shepherd,' Jesus explained. 'I really care about my sheep. A hired worker does not care about the sheep. He cares more about his own safety and soon runs off if a wolf attacks the lambs.

'I know and care for every single one who belongs to me, as a good shepherd does for every lamb in his flock. My sheep know me too. They listen when I call and follow me in the right way.

'I love my sheep so much that I am going to die for them. But just as certainly as I am going to give my life, I shall take it back again.

'One day I shall gather up all the other sheep still wandering in the world who belong to me. They will come safely into my sheepfold and be part of one huge flock.'

Short cut through Samaria

The shortest route from Jerusalem to the north lay through the province of Samaria. But Jews who were strict about keeping God's law preferred to take a much longer route, rather than go that way. They despised the Samaritans, who were half-cast foreigners, and would have nothing to do with them.

Centuries before, the Jews had intermarried with people whom the conquering Assyrians had settled in

can you ask *me* for a drink?'

Jesus looked up. He knew all about her unhappy life. He knew how badly she needed God's forgiveness and joy.

'If you knew who I am and what God wants to give you, you would ask *me* for a drink,' he told her. 'I would give you life-giving water, that would quench your thirst for ever!'

'That sounds wonderful,' she joked. 'It would save me the trouble of coming to this well every day!'

But when she discovered that Jesus knew all the details of her life story, she stopped joking and pretending. By the time the astonished disciples had arrived back, she had recognized Jesus as the Messiah that Samaritans as well as Jews were waiting for.

She scurried off to tell the townspeople about the wonderful Jewish teacher, who knew everything about her and cared for Samaritans as well as the chosen Jewish people. Soon they were hurrying to the well to hear him for themselves.

Meanwhile the disciples stared in amazement at their Master. They could not believe that he was ready to give his time and care to a disreputable woman who belonged to the despised Samaritan race.

The man who said 'Thank you!'

Near the border of Samaria and Galilee, Jesus saw a bunch of ten thin and ragged men, hovering on the outskirts of the village. They looked longingly across at him, but dared not come closer. They were forbidden by law to mix with other people, because of the skin disease from which they suffered.

Perhaps they had heard how Jesus had healed others with the same disease, because they shouted to him, 'Jesus!

their land. The mixed race that lived there now had their own version of the Jewish faith and their own holy places.

But Jesus led his disciples through Samaria, and at noon, when the sun was hottest, they arrived at the Samaritan town of Sychar. The disciples set off to buy food, while Jesus sat on the edge of the well, just outside the town. He was tired and very thirsty.

Soon a Samaritan woman came slowly towards the well, carrying her empty water pot.

'Would you give me a drink, please?' Jesus asked.

The woman could hardly believe her ears. To think that a Jew would talk to a woman—and a Samaritan at that! As for asking for a drink—no Jew would drink from the cup a Samaritan had used.

'You are a Jew,' she blurted out. 'How

Master! Have pity on us!'

Jesus looked at them with great kindness. Then he said, 'Go straight to the priests and let them examine you.'

That could mean only one thing, they knew. It was the priest's job to declare a patient free from infection.

They scrambled and hobbled off, as fast as they could go, without a word. As they went, every man noticed, with amazement and delight, that his deformed limbs had grown straight and strong again, and that his sores had healed, leaving the skin fresh and unmarked once more.

They laughed and shouted and leaped and sang for joy.

But one of them, a Samaritan, suddenly stopped. He stood quite still, then turned back, running towards Jesus. He went right up to him and threw himself, breathless, at Jesus' feet.

'Thank you, Master!' he blurted out. 'Thank you for healing me!'

'Where are the others?' Jesus asked. 'There were ten of you. Where are the other nine?' The man said nothing.

'You are a Samaritan,' Jesus went on, 'with none of the advantages of God's chosen people. Yet you are the only one who has come back to give thanks to God.'

Then he bent gently down to him. 'Get up!' he told him, 'and be on your way. Your faith has made you well.'

Lost and Found

Jesus was surrounded, as he often was, by the kind of people the religious leaders looked down on.

'This man seems to welcome sinners!' one Pharisee said.

'He even goes to dinner with them!' another added.

So Jesus told three stories, to help them understand how God felt about the people they despised.

THE STORY OF THE LOST SHEEP

Imagine that you own a hundred sheep. One day, when you count them, one is missing. You don't stop for a moment, but leave the other ninety-nine in the field and set off to look for that one lost sheep.

And when you find it—what joy! You put it on your shoulders and hurry back. You tell everyone the good news and invite your friends in to share your happiness.

You can be sure that there is more joy in heaven over one sinner who turns back to God than over ninety-nine respectable people who see no need to repent.

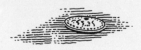

THE STORY OF THE LOST COIN

You women, imagine that you have lost one of your ten precious silver pieces!

You light a lamp, sweep the floor and search high and low until, at last, you see it gleaming in some dark corner. You are so excited that you go into the courtyard and call out to everyone to come and celebrate with you, because you have found your lost coin.

It is just like that in heaven. The angels of God celebrate when one sinner turns back to God.

109

There was once a farmer who had two sons. One day, the younger son said to him, 'Father, will you give me my share of your property?'

So his father divided all he owned and gave his son the share that would be his. The young man sold it, then left home with a light heart and a full purse.

But he spent his money recklessly in a far off country, and before long he was down to his last coin. Worse still, there was a famine where he was living, so everyone was poor and short of food.

At last he got a job—looking after pigs. He was so hungry that he would gladly have eaten the bean pods he fed to them. But no one gave him anything.

At last he came to his senses.

'Here I am, almost starving,' he said to himself, 'yet my father's hired workers get more to eat than they need. I will go home and tell my father how wrong and foolish I have been, and ask him to give me a job.'

So he set off on the journey back.

But when he was still a long way off, his father saw him and ran to meet him. With tears of joy, he threw his arms around him and kissed him.

'Father,' his son began, 'I have sinned against God and against you. I am not fit to be your son.'

But his father would not let him go on. He began shouting excited orders to the startled servants:

'Hurry up and fetch the best robe I've got—and some new sandals—and my ring,' he told one, while to another he said, 'Kill that calf we've been fattening and prepare a splendid feast. We must celebrate!'

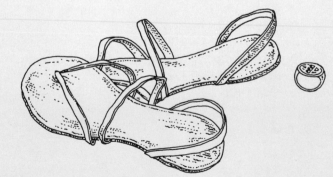

When his older son came home from the fields, he heard the sound of music and dancing and laughter.

'What's happening?' he asked one of the servants.

'The master is giving a feast for your brother,' the servant explained. 'He's home, safe and sound.'

The older son was furious and refused to go into the house. His father came out to persuade him to join in the celebrations. But he said angrily:

'I've worked like a slave for you all these years and you have never even offered me a goat for a feast with my friends! Now this good-for-nothing son of yours, who has wasted your money, turns up like a bad penny, and you kill the prize calf for him!'

'My son,' his father said gently, 'you are with me all the time and everything I own will be yours. Isn't it right that we should be happy and celebrate? Your brother was "dead", but now he's alive. He was lost and now he is found!'

At the time of Jesus, sheep were important providers of wool and meat, milk and cheese. They were in demand as temple offerings too. Pasture was poor on the hills, so the shepherd had to move the flock from place to place. Unlike most shepherds today, he did not drive the flock, but led it: he knew each of his sheep, and they knew and answered to his call. He searched for any sheep that strayed, and rescued them from dangerous places. He protected the sheep from wild animals and from thieves, using his catapult or wooden club. At night he led the sheep into a stone-walled sheepfold, topped with thorns—and lay across the entrance himself to keep them safe.

CHAPTER 15

Enemies in the Camp

'Isn't Jesus wonderful?' someone in the crowd murmured. He gazed at the calm, happy face of a man who, minutes before, had been wild and terrified, unable to see or speak.

'He must be the Messiah, God's promised King,' his friend replied. 'He's the only one who could cast out evil the way he does.'

A group of Pharisees overheard them.

'Nothing of the kind!' one of them snapped. 'It's more like black magic. Jesus uses the Devil's own powers to cast out demons.'

Jesus turned to them and said, 'What happens when members of the same family start quarrelling? Or if civil war breaks out in a country? Doesn't it spell disaster? That family—or country— falls apart. Satan is not foolish enough to fight against himself and cast out his own demons.

'It is by the power of God that I cast out demons, sure proof that God's kingdom has arrived! To see God at work and believe it is the work of Satan—that is a sin that can never be forgiven.'

'Arrest that man!'

The Pharisees and religious leaders could not bear to hear the ordinary people praising Jesus and suggesting that he might be the Messiah. They were bitterly jealous. So they sent some of their guards to arrest Jesus and bring him to them.

The soldiers arrived and awaited their chance on the outskirts of the crowd. But the longer they listened, the more they were drawn to Jesus and to what he said and did.

In the end, they went back without their prisoner.

'Where is he?' the priests and leaders asked. 'Why haven't you brought him?'

'We never heard anyone talk the way he does!' the soldiers answered.

'So he fooled you, too?' the priests asked in contempt. 'No one who matters believes him or follows him. The common people may run after him, but they don't even know the law of Moses, so they are under God's curse.'

But one of the Pharisees, Nicodemus, took a different view. He had talked with Jesus alone, one memorable night. Although he had not become his follower openly, he was certain that Jesus spoke the truth.

Jesus was no ordinary teacher. He had come from God with God's own message. He had told him—Nicodemus, a religious leader—that he needed to become as unimportant as a child and be born into God's family, if he was to be part of God's kingdom. And Nicodemus knew that he was right.

'I don't think we should condemn a man without giving him a chance to defend himself,' he said cautiously.

'So you are one of his followers, too,' one of his colleagues remarked, sarcastically. 'Who ever heard of a prophet coming from Galilee?'

Watch out for hypocrites!

Jesus began to warn his followers to be on their guard against the Pharisees.

'It's the job of the Pharisees and the religious teachers to explain the law to you,' he said, 'so you must listen to what they say. But don't follow their example because they don't do what they preach. They just want to attract attention to themselves and be made a fuss of wherever they go. But the person who is greatest in my kingdom is the one who is ready to be unimportant, and go unnoticed by others.'

One of the Pharisees, who had been listening, invited Jesus to dinner. Jesus did not make a ceremony of washing beforehand, as his host did, and the Pharisee showed his surprise and disapproval.

'I know how fussy you Pharisees are about washing hands and cups and plates,' Jesus said. 'But how clean are your hearts and minds? You are fools if you think that God can be fobbed off with outward cleanliness! He looks for clean and wholesome lives. Give the food on your plates to the hungry. That will make you clean in God's sight!

'You put aside one tenth of everything you have for God, down to the herbs in your garden,' Jesus went on, 'but you brush aside the important commands of God—that you should give the poor a fair deal, and help those who cannot help themselves!'

One of the teachers the law remarked, 'Teacher, when you talk like that you insult us, too!'

'Yes, you are just as guilty,' Jesus agreed. 'You will be severely judged, because instead of bearing the burdens of the ordinary people, you make life doubly hard for them with all your petty rules and regulations. You put heavy loads on their backs, telling them all the things they ought to do, but you don't lift a finger to help them. You keep to yourselves the key to knowing God. How terrible it will be for you all on God's judgment day!'

When Jesus left, the religious leaders broke into angry discussion. Somehow they must prove him wrong.

Interruptions on the Way

Wherever Jesus went, he met with interruptions. Someone was sure to stop him to ask if he would heal their friend or settle their arguments. And he always found time for those who came to him for help.

One day, Jesus and his friends were on their way back to Capernaum, followed by the usual jostling crowd, when a little group of people came hurrying up. They pointed to the frightened man they were bringing to Jesus.

'He can't hear!' one of them explained.

'He can't talk properly, either,' another added.

'So please can you help him?' they asked.

Jesus looked from the faces of the friends to the anxious face of the man himself. He realized how confused he must feel, to be part of a noisy crowd without being able to hear or make himself understood. Quickly he led him away from the other people.

When they were on their own, Jesus put his fingers first in the man's ears, then on his tongue, to help him understand by signs what he was going to do. Then he looked upwards, to show that he was asking God for help. He spoke one word: 'Ephphatha,' which means 'Open up!'

At once, the man was able to hear perfectly. He found that he could talk clearly too. His friends arrived, delighted to hear him praising God and thanking Jesus.

The key to life

Sometimes the disciples were surprised that Jesus seemed to take more trouble with women and children, or dirty, smelly beggars than he did with well-dressed men and religious leaders. Everyone mattered to him, but especially those who needed his help.

That day, though, the man who came running towards them along the dusty road was young, handsome and wealthy. The disciples were amazed when he knelt breathless before Jesus, dragging his fine clothes in the dust.

'Good Master,' he began, 'how can I gain eternal life?'

Jesus looked at the real person beneath the rich clothes and flattering words.

'Why do you call me good?' he asked.

'Only God is good.' Then he went on, 'You know the commandments by heart. Obey them—that is the key to life.'

'But I've kept all the commandments since I was a boy,' the young man protested, impatiently.

Jesus looked at him with warmth and affection. He knew that he had indeed lived a moral life. But he had not understood that the key to keeping God's law is to love God above everything else.

'There is one more thing you must do,' Jesus told him. 'Sell everything you own and give the money to the poor. Then you will be really rich—in God's eyes. After that, come and follow me.'

A dark shadow crossed the young man's face. He loved his house and land, his clothes and jewels. He turned away, heavy-hearted, and trudged slowly back along the road he had come.

'How hard it is for rich people to enter God's kingdom!' Jesus told the disciples. They could not believe their ears. That was not what they thought.

'But aren't rich people the ones that God has specially blessed?' they asked. 'If *they* can't be saved, whoever can?'

'No one—rich or poor—can be saved by their own efforts,' Jesus told them. 'But with God everything is possible,' he added with certainty.

'Don't cry!'

As Jesus trudged up the hill towards the town of Nain, followed by a chattering, excited mob, they met a little procession at the town gates. It was on its way down the narrow path towards them, heading for the rocky caves in the hills where the townsfolk buried their dead.

They could hear the shrill cries and moans of the mourners. They accompanied the heartbroken woman as she walked beside the stretcher, where her dead son lay. Jesus knew that she had no husband and no other son to keep her or take care of her. His heart went out to her.

'Don't cry!' he told her. Then he went over to the stretcher and put his hand on it. The men who were carrying it stopped still. To their amazement, Jesus spoke to the lifeless corpse: 'Young man!' he said. 'Wake up!'

The still figure stirred, sat bolt upright and at once began to talk. Jesus helped him to his feet and took him across to his mother, gently handing him back into her care.

The onlookers were amazed.

'God has surely come to save us!' someone piously exclaimed.

Stories about Money

'Please tell my brother to give me my fair share of our inheritance,' a man in the crowd asked Jesus one day.

'My friend, it is not for me to settle family arguments,' Jesus told him. *'But don't be greedy. What a person is worth has nothing to do with how much he owns.'*

THE FOOLISH FARMER

There was once a farmer who had a bumper harvest. So he sat down and planned his future.

'I'll pull down my barns,' he decided, 'and build bigger ones. Then I can store all my crops and sit back. I have enough saved up to keep me in luxury for years to come!'

But God said to that farmer, 'What a fool you are! Tonight you are going to die! What good will all your money do you then?'

That's the way it is with people who pile up money for themselves and forget to care for others and give to them. That is the way to be rich by God's reckoning.

THE MAN WHO MADE MONEY HIS FRIEND

One day, a wealthy estate owner discovered that his manager was wasting his money.

'I'm giving you notice,' he told him sternly, 'so get the books straight and hand them over to me.'

'What am I going to do?' thought the farm manager. 'I'm not tough enough to work on the land and I'm too proud to beg. I know what I'll do! I'll find a way of making friends to look after me once I'm out of a job.'

He sent for everyone who owed his master money.

'How much do you owe?' he asked the first one.

'A hundred barrels of olive oil,' the man answered.

'Sit down here and change that to fifty,' the manager told him.

'What do you owe?' he asked the next man.

'A thousand sacks of wheat,' he replied.

'Change that to eighty,' he told him.

His employer heard about it and admired his cunning.

'You're a clever chap!' he told him.

> 'People who don't care about God's kingdom often show more enterprise in handling money than you do,' Jesus told his followers. 'Learn to use money well, to help others, then God will trust you with real riches.'

CHAPTER 17

The Gift of Life

Whenever Jesus went to Jerusalem, he would visit his friends, Martha and Mary and their brother Lazarus, who lived in the village of Bethany, close to the city.

One day, Jesus received an urgent message, sent by the two sisters:

'Lord, your friend Lazarus is ill.'

'This illness won't end in death, but it will bring glory to God,' Jesus reassured the disciples.

They were comforted by what he said, but concerned that he would want to go straight to Bethany to heal Lazarus. Last time they had been in Judea, Jesus' life had been threatened. But, to their surprise, two whole days passed before Jesus said, 'It's time, now, to go to Judea.'

'You know what happened last time we were there,' the disciples reminded him. 'They wanted to stone you.'

'All the same, if the Master has decided to go, we'll go too,' Thomas insisted. 'We'll die with him, if need be!'

'No one can harm me while I still have work to do for my Father,' Jesus assured them. 'He has given me a certain time for my work—that's like the day. Daylight is safe. It's at night that you trip over and hurt yourself. But the night will come,' he added.

As they walked the rough road, Jesus told them, 'Our friend Lazarus is asleep.'

'Then he must be getting better,' the disciples said cheerfully.

'I mean that he is sleeping the sleep of death,' Jesus explained. 'Lazarus is dead.'

The disciples fell silent. Once more they were puzzled by their Master.

The Lord of life

Bad news travels fast. Before Jesus and his friends arrived, someone told them the news, 'You're too late! Lazarus has been dead and buried four whole days!'

When they were in sight of the house, they could see little groups of people arriving, to comfort the sisters and sympathize with them in their sadness.

When Martha heard that Jesus was on his way, she hurried out of the house to meet him.

'If only you had been here,' she burst out, 'Lazarus would be alive today!' Then she added, more thoughtfully, 'But I know that even now God will hear your prayers.'

'Martha, dear,' Jesus said confidently, 'your brother will rise to life. I am the resurrection and I am life. Everyone who puts faith in me will live for ever, even though the body dies. Do you believe this?'

'Yes, Lord!' Martha answered through her tears. 'I believe that you are God's Messiah!'

Martha went quickly back home to tell Mary to go to Jesus before he reached the crowded house. But when Mary got up to go, her visitors followed, thinking she was going to Lazarus' grave, to mourn there.

When Jesus saw Mary's tears and the tears of the friends who were with her, he cried too. He felt very sad to see them so unhappy. He was angry, too, as he saw the pain and sorrow death brings, spoiling God's plans for life and family happiness.

'Where is Lazarus buried?' he asked.

'Come and see,' they said, leading the way to the rock tomb.

When they arrived, Jesus ordered, 'Take away the stone that blocks the entrance.'

123

Everyone was shocked and Martha protested. 'We can't do that! He's been dead four days. The body will smell.'

'Remember what I told you,' Jesus said. 'If you trust me, you will see God act in great power.'

So, at a nod from the sisters, one or two strong men hauled the heavy rock from the cave mouth. No one else moved in the hot, still air.

Jesus looked upwards and said, 'Thank you, Father, for listening to me. I know that you always do.'

Then, in a loud voice, he gave the command: 'Come out, Lazarus!'

Everyone held their breath. Curiosity and fear were on every face. All eyes were fastened on the shadowy, dark interior of the cave. Then, from within, a white, shrouded figure emerged uncertainly into the bright sunlight, body and head bound tightly by the linen bands of the burial shroud.

'Unloose the burial clothes! Set him free!' Jesus said.

Loving, flustered hands hastened to unwind the cloths. Lazarus stretched, smiled, then strode out healthy and whole.

'Let Jesus die!'

Everyone was talking about the man who had come back to life. Some felt certain now that Jesus really was sent by God and put full faith in him.

But others hurried off to Jerusalem to pass on the news of Jesus' latest miracle to his enemies.

An urgent meeting of the Council was called and the members members discussed with the leading priests and Pharisees what to do about Jesus.

'We must take action quickly,' they decided. 'The crowds are flocking after him and he'll soon be everyone's hero. That will be a disaster for us all. It could cause trouble with Rome, too.'

Caiaphas, the High Priest, interrupted their chatter.

'Don't be a pack of fools!' he said coolly. 'Can't you see the obvious solution? Get rid of Jesus! It's far better for one man to die than for all of us to suffer.'

He did not realize how true his words were. Jesus was indeed going to suffer and die on behalf of everyone else.

From that day on, the Jewish authorities began to make plans to bring about Jesus' death.

When they heard that Bethany was buzzing with crowds of sightseers, all coming to stare at the man who had come back from the dead, they even talked of getting rid of Lazarus too, to destroy the evidence.

Meanwhile Jesus and the disciples left the danger zone. Jesus knew there was still work for him to do before God's appointed time for him to die.

*Jesus often used the title 'Son of man' for himself. The
Book of Daniel in the Scriptures described the Son of
man as the one God has chosen to rule and judge all
people everywhere. One day Jesus told this story . . .*

When the Son of man comes as King, with all his angel host, he will
separate mankind into two groups, just as a shepherd divides the
sheep from the goats in his flock. He will say to those on his right, 'Come
and possess the kingdom made ready for you! God's blessing is on you.
When I was hungry you fed me, and when I was thirsty you gave me a
drink. I was a stranger and you took me into your homes, naked and you
gave me clothes; I was sick and you took care of me; I was in prison and
you visited me.'

The righteous people were puzzled. They said, 'Lord, we never saw
you hungry or thirsty, homeless or ill, or in prison, and took care of you.'

'But whenever you did these things for one of the least important of
my people, you were doing it for me,' the King told them.

Then he turned to those on his left.

'Go right away from me,' he said sternly. 'When I was hungry you did
not feed me, and you gave me no water when I was thirsty. When I was a
stranger you did not welcome me home. I was naked but you gave me
no clothes; I was ill and in prison but you did not look after me.'

These people were puzzled too and protested, 'We never saw you in
need and refused to help you!'

'Whenever you refused to help any of the least important of my
people,' the King told them, 'you were refusing to help me.'

*Jesus ended with these solemn words: 'Their future
will be eternal punishment but the righteous will enjoy
eternal life.'*

CHAPTER 18

The Road to Jerusalem

Spring was coming and preparations were afoot, in the towns and villages, for the annual expedition to Jerusalem. Soon it would be time to go and celebrate Passover.

But, as Jesus led his disciples along the road, no one was feeling excited or in holiday mood. The Master pressed forward with such determination and urgency that their hearts were gripped by fear and foreboding. He did not behave like a triumphant king going to be crowned. He seemed to be facing some terrible ordeal. Instinctively, they lagged behind, leaving him to walk ahead, alone.

They were sure that their Master was God's chosen King, the Messiah who had come to bring in God's rule of justice and love. So why did he keep talking as if nothing but suffering and death lay in store for him?

Even the crowds that trailed after them seemed to sense the solemn mood. They felt afraid, without knowing what they were frightened of.

After a while, Jesus stopped and waited for his twelve friends to catch up with him. Then he drew them aside and talked to them, quietly but urgently:

'Listen!' he said. 'We are on our way to Jerusalem. When we get there I shall be arrested and handed over to the chief priests and teachers of the law. They will pass the death sentence on me and hand me over to the Romans. I shall be jeered at and whipped, then put to death by crucifixion. But that will not be the end.

In three days I shall be raised to life again.'

The disciples looked at one another in utter dismay. Each time he told them about dying he added more dreadful details. They had no idea what he was talking about and they did not want to think about it. But they were determined to follow him loyally, whatever the end of that journey might bring.

Rich man in hiding

Jericho, the city of palm-trees, was a welcome stage on the road to Jerusalem. It was good to walk along the tree-lined street, to feast the eyes on bright flowering shrubs and enjoy the bustle of a prosperous and beautiful city.

Tax collectors in Jericho found especially rich pickings and none did better than Zacchaeus, who was in charge of tax collecting in the city. He was wealthy and owned a fine house. But his job left him with few respectable friends.

When Zacchaeus knew that Jesus was coming to Jericho he made up his mind to see him. Rumour had it that Jesus had chosen a tax collector as one of his closest friends. This teacher sounded very different from the proud and condemning rabbis who always ignored or insulted him.

He could see the crowd of pilgrims winding their way slowly along the road through the city. Most of the citizens of Jericho seemed to have turned out to welcome them. Zacchaeus was very

short. He would never be able to see over their heads, to get a glimpse of Jesus.

He glanced appraisingly at the sycomore fig-tree beside the road. He was still agile enough to climb it. In a moment he had shinned up the lower branches and settled himself in a convenient fork, where he could see everything and be seen by no one.

As the procession came nearer, Zacchaeus concentrated his gaze on Jesus, the person at the heart of the crowd. But he could see only the top of his head. If only he could look into his face!

At that moment, as if his wish had been heard, Jesus stopped beneath the tree and gazed up into the branches.

'Hurry down, Zacchaeus!' he called out. 'I want to come to your home.'

Zacchaeus' feet touched ground at record speed. His usually tense, unhappy face lit up with a broad smile as he said, 'Welcome, Master! Come with me!'

But there was a murmur of disapproval from the crowd.

'You'd think there were enough decent folk in Jericho; why must he go to dinner with a man like that!' they muttered.

Zacchaeus no longer heard or cared for their comments. Jesus' love and acceptance made him feel warm and happy. But being with Jesus also made him ashamed of his meanness and dishonesty.

No one heard what Jesus said to Zacchaeus in the cool luxury of the house, but when they came outside again to the waiting crowd Zacchaeus announced, 'I want to put right the wrongs that I have done. I'm going to give half of everything I own to the poor. And where I have taken too much money in taxes from anyone, I shall pay them back four times over.'

Some of the local people stared in disbelief. Others looked at Zacchaeus with contempt. But Jesus told them: 'Salvation has come to Zacchaeus' house today. He is truly one of God's children. Don't forget! The very reason I came to this world is to find and rescue those who have strayed away from God.'

The beggar by the roadside

Even prosperous Jericho had its share of beggars. As Jesus and the disciples were leaving the city, they could hear, above the hubbub of the crowd, someone shouting, 'Jesus! Son of David! Have pity on me!'

129

They looked to see where the noise was coming from, and recognized Bartimaeus, the blind beggar, who always sat by the roadside with his begging bowl. But now he was on his feet, waving his arms excitedly and shouting over and over again, 'Have pity on me, Jesus, son of David!'

Everyone was saying 'Shush!', 'Stop being a nuisance!', but he took no notice—shouting even louder.

Jesus stood still.

'Tell him to come to me,' he said. The message buzzed along the bystanders and those nearest to Bartimaeus, the first to try to silence him, now told him to cheer up and go to Jesus.

Bartimaeus threw off his tattered cloak and, guided by willing hands, made his way to the middle of the crowd, where Jesus was waiting for him.

'What do you want me to do for you?' Jesus asked.

He knew that Bartimaeus' life would change completely if he could see. He would no longer be able to earn his living as a beggar. But Bartimaeus had no second thoughts.

'Teacher,' he answered eagerly, 'I want to see!'

'Your faith in me has made you well,' Jesus said. 'Off you go now. You will be able to see.'

But when Bartimaeus looked, with new-found sight, into Jesus' face, he did not want to go away. He had discovered the Messiah, the son of David, for himself. Now he would follow him wherever he went.

The Rich Man and the Beggar

*'A slave can never serve two different masters,' Jesus
said; 'it is impossible to be all out for God and all out
for money too.'*

*The Pharisees sneered at Jesus because they thought
they could have religion and money too.*

So Jesus told this story . . .

There was once a very rich man. He dressed in the most expensive
clothes that money could buy and ate rich, luxury meals every day
of the week.

There was also a very poor beggar, called Lazarus, whose rags
scarcely covered his sores. He used to be brought to the rich man's door,
in the hope that the hunks of bread, on which the rich man wiped his
fingers, might come his way. The scavenger dogs licked his sores.

One day Lazarus died and angels carried him to feast in heaven beside
Abraham. The rich man died too and went to the world of the dead. He
could see Lazarus in bliss, and he cried out in his pain, 'Please, Father
Abraham, send Lazarus to cool my tongue with water!'

But Abraham replied, 'My son, remember how you once had all the
good things in life, while Lazarus had none. Now he is happy while you
are in pain. But he cannot help you, for there is a great pit between us
that no one can cross.'

'Then please send Lazarus back to earth to warn my five brothers not
to end up as I have done.'

'Your brothers have the books of Moses and the prophets,' Abraham
reminded him. 'They can take heed of their warnings.'

'But if someone went to them from the dead, that would make them
listen,' the rich man persisted.

'If they won't take any notice of the Scriptures,' Abraham told him
solemnly, 'they won't be convinced, even if someone comes back from
the dead.'

The white and gold temple rebuilt by King Herod the Great was the centre of Jewish worship in Jesus' day. People crowded into Jerusalem at festival times.

The temple courtyards were full of worshipers bringing their offerings. In the shady colonnades all around, the rabbis taught groups of their followers.

The outer court was open to everyone, but notices forbade those who were not Jews from going further—on pain of death.

Inside were the Court of the Women, then the Court of the Men of Israel, then the Court of the Priests.

At the very centre was the temple itself: a house built for God. It had an outer room, where the priests took turns to burn incense, keep the lamps alight on the great lampstand, and put bread on the table.

The inner room was unlit: it was God's private, holy place. The high priest was the only one allowed in—just once a year, on the Day of Atonement for the wrongdoings of the people.

Court
the Pri

Outer courtyard
– *open to everyone*

Outer courtyard
– *open to everyone*

Court of the   Men of Israel

Altar

Offering box

Court of the Women

CHAPTER 19

Here Comes the King!

The long, uphill trudge from Jericho to Jerusalem, where bare, forbidding rocks overhung their path, was over at last. Now, from the pleasant slope of the Mount of Olives, they could gaze across the valley to the holy city, their eyes dazzled by the gleaming temple.

Before they had arrived at this vantage point, Jesus sent two of the disciples on ahead to a nearby village.

'On the way in, you will see a young donkey, tethered beside its mother,' Jesus told them. 'Bring it here to me. If anyone asks you why you are taking the donkey away, just tell them that the Master needs it.'

The two friends found the little donkey and, when they told the villagers that the Master wanted it, no one seemed to mind them leading it off. The disciples realized, once more, that Jesus had more friends—and plans—than they knew about.

The donkey had not yet been broken in, and the two disciples had to coax it along. But as soon as Jesus put his hand on the donkey's neck it was quiet.

Some of the disciples threw their cloaks on to its back, for a makeshift saddle, and Jesus climbed on. Then, with a cheer, the whole party set off down the steep path, through the olive groves, into the valley at the foot of Jerusalem.

When they began the steep climb up the other side, into the city, they saw a stream of Passover pilgrims pouring out to meet them. These early arrivals had found Jerusalem buzzing with news. Everyone was talking about how Jesus had brought Lazarus back from the dead. They were eager to see this miracle worker. As the two crowds met, there was a burst of cheering.

Some of the pilgrims tore down branches from the palm-trees that lined the road and laid them down to make a path for Jesus. Others spread their

cloaks as a royal carpet for Jesus to ride on. Someone began singing an old hymn of praise to God for his Messiah. One after another began to join in the words, as they sang exuberantly:

'God bless the one who comes in the
    name of the Lord!
Praise to David's son!'

The disciples were as excited as everyone else. Later on they remembered what the prophet Zechariah had written centuries before:

'Shout for joy, you people of
    Jerusalem!
Look, your king is coming to you!
He comes triumphant and victorious,
but humble, and riding on a donkey.'

Jesus had found a way to tell the crowds he was the Messiah—and a

peacemaking king—without speaking a word.

The Pharisees were furious; disgusted by the crowd's demonstration. Some of them complained.

'Can't you tell your followers to be quiet?' they asked with cold anger.

But Jesus replied, 'If they were silent, these stones would shout out!'

The twelve disciples were delighted that, at last, the Master was getting the recognition he deserved. The secret was out! Now everyone knew that Jesus was

David's son, the promised Messiah. Surely, everything would turn out all right after all. In no time he would be crowned King!

If only . . .!

Jesus and the Twelve, like other pilgrims in overcrowded Jerusalem, stayed the nights of Passover week in Bethany, walking down the Mount of Olives and up to the city each day.

One morning, as Jesus looked across at Jerusalem from the Mount of Olives, sadness welled up inside him and he wept as if his heart would break.

'O Jerusalem!' he cried. 'How often I have longed to gather all your people safely around me—as a mother hen gathers her chicks under her wing! If only I could save you from the terrible disasters that are coming! But you won't let me! You don't understand that I could bring you peace. God's hour has arrived but you don't recognize this as the time when you could be saved.'

The disciples were gazing in wonder at the magnificent temple buildings.

'Look at those colossal stones, Master!' one of them said admiringly.

'What a fantastic building it is!' another added.

Jesus shook his head sadly. 'Look hard!' Jesus told them. 'Because the time is coming soon when not one of those stones will be left in place. Every one of them will be torn down.'

The disciples said nothing then. They felt too bothered and upset. But later on the brothers Peter and Andrew, with James and John, asked Jesus in private what he meant when he talked about the temple being pulled down.

'It's true,' he repeated. 'Terrible times are in store. You will be badly treated because you are my followers. And this temple will be invaded by those without reverence for God. Jerusalem itself will be under siege. Those who are wise will watch for the warning signs and get out of the city as fast as they can.

'Another day of judgment is coming

one day too. I, the Son of man, will come back to this world in glory and power. My angels will spread out to the four corners of the world, to gather my chosen people together and bring them to me.'

Cheating in the house of God!

Jesus and the disciples climbed the wide steps and entered the gate leading to the outermost temple courtyard. This was the only part of the temple where non-Jews were allowed.

They were met by a medley of noises and smells. Sheep and goats were tethered there, and caged birds too, all on sale for sacrifice. There were stalls where money-changers, who provided temple coinage to pay the temple tax, were haggling and cheating their customers. Laden city dwellers criss-crossed the surging crowds, using the court as a short-cut. All was pandemonium.

As Jesus looked around he felt very angry. This court was the one place in all the world where those who did not know the true God could come to pray and learn about him. Instead, they would be cheated and robbed.

He strode between the crowded ranks of stalls, sending tables flying. Coins rolled everywhere, to the consternation of the money-changers. Then he drove the animals out through the gates and shouted to the men who sold pigeons,

'Take them out of here!' The people taking a short cut through the court with their baggage were sent packing.

Then he spoke to them all.

'God says that his house is to be a place of prayer. But look what you have turned it into! It's no better than a thieves' hideout!'

Only the rich and dishonest traders were afraid of Jesus. The poor people were glad to see those who cheated them turned out, and order restored to God's court. The sick and disabled made their way as fast as they could to where Jesus stood. He was their champion and rescuer. And Jesus healed them all.

The fig-tree without any figs

When Jesus was going into the city early next morning, he felt very hungry. He stopped beside a fig-tree and peered into its branches but there was no fruit to be seen.

The fig-tree was often used as a picture of the Jewish nation. Just as Jesus longed for fruit on this tree, so, down the ages, God had longed to see the good fruit of justice and kindness in the life of the nation. But they had refused to listen to the warnings of God's messengers, the prophets. Now they were resisting Jesus, God's chosen King.

Earlier on, Jesus had told a story about a fig-tree which bore no fruit, year after year. The owner decided to cut it down, but his gardener begged, 'Give it one more chance! I'll dig around it and give it fertilizer. If it still has no fruit next year, then cut it down. But who knows—it may have figs!'

Now Jesus spoke to the tree in front of him: 'Never again will you have figs!' he pronounced.

The disciples looked on in amazement. The tree seemed to wither before their eyes.

How Jesus had longed to see his people bear fruit by receiving God and his King! But now it was too late. In spite of all that he had said and done, they had said 'No!' once too often.

Be Ready!

When Jesus came to our world, many of his own people were not ready to welcome him. Jesus knew that many people will not be ready for him when he comes back again. So he told some stories to remind everyone to be ready for God's King and to explain how to prepare for his coming—even though it is as unexpected as a burglar's visit in the middle of the night!

THE STORY OF THE TEN BRIDESMAIDS

Ten girls set out one night to a wedding, to wait for the bridegroom's torchlight procession. All took their lamps, but only five were wise enough to take a good supply of oil.

They had a long time to wait, so they dozed, then fell fast asleep.

Suddenly, at midnight, they woke with a start.

'Here comes the bridegroom! Come and meet him!' everyone was shouting.

They scrambled to their feet and hurriedly trimmed their lamps. Then the five foolish ones realized that their oil had run out and they had no supplies.

'Will you lend us some oil?' they asked the others.

But the five sensible girls had only enough for themselves. So the foolish girls had to hurry off to look for a shop that was still open.

Meanwhile the procession reached the bridegroom's home and everyone went in to feast and have fun.

The foolish girls arrived at last, knocking on the dark door and begging to be let in. But they were too late. They missed the joy of the wedding feast.

THE STORY OF THE THREE SERVANTS

There was once a man who had to go on a long journey, so he left his servants in charge of all he owned. He gave five thousand gold coins to the first one, two thousand to the next and one thousand to the third.

The first two worked very hard while their master was away and made a good profit by trading with his gold. But the third one did no work. He wrapped up the coins, dug a hole in the ground and buried them.

At long last the master arrived home.

'How have you all managed?' he asked his servants.

'I've doubled what you left with me,' the first one said, handing over the extra ten thousand gold coins.

'Well done!' the master exclaimed. 'You have been a good, trustworthy servant. I shall give you a more responsible job now. Come and share my happiness!'

'I've earned double too,' the second servant told him, and his master praised him just as much.

Then he turned to the third servant, who was scowling in the corner, and asked how he had done.

'I know you are a hard, mean man,' that servant said. 'I was afraid to risk losing your money. So I hid it instead. Here you are—you can have it back.' And he handed over the bag of coins.

His master was angry.

'If I'm such a skinflint you could at least have put my money in the bank to earn interest. But the truth is that you are just a lazy, bad servant. Get out!'

Then he ordered the thousand gold coins to be given to the servant who had made the most money.

'For those who make full use of whatever they have been given,' Jesus added, 'will end up with even more.'

CHAPTER 20

Questions and Answers

The leading priests and religious teachers were itching to get their hands on Jesus and put him out of the way for ever. But they were afraid of upsetting the ordinary people who loved him. They would have to look for a very good reason to have him arrested.

If Jesus could be persuaded to speak out against the Romans, he would be handed over to the Roman Governor. If they could trap him into making this sort of mistake he would be signing his own death warrant.

Rather than question Jesus themselves, they bribed some men to join the crowd and ask their question for them.

They said: 'Teacher, we know that you always speak the truth no matter what others think. Please tell us whether we ought to pay taxes to the Romans.'

No good Jew liked having to pay the Roman taxes. If Jesus said they ought to pay, he would be very unpopular. But if he told the people not to pay them, they could get him into trouble with the Romans.

Jesus saw through the trick.

'Has anyone a silver coin to show me?' he asked.

Someone in the crowd produced one from his money bag and handed it to Jesus. He held it up and asked, 'Whose head is on the coin?'

'The Emperor's,' those nearby answered.

'Then pay the Emperor what is due to him,' Jesus told them. 'But give God, too, what is owing to *him*.'

The Sadducees, who did not believe in life after death, were the next to ask a question. They hoped to make Jesus look silly by proving that no sensible person could believe in resurrection.

'There were once seven brothers,' they began. 'The eldest got married, but he died. So his brother married the widow, as our law says he should. He died too. In fact, all seven of them married her and they all died. The woman died last of all. Now please tell us which one of them will be her husband in the life to come.'

'You've got it all wrong,' Jesus explained. 'The next world will not be an exact copy of this one. Men and women will be changed. They won't need to marry and have children but will live as the angels do.

'But there *is* a life after death,' he went on. 'The Scriptures themselves prove it. When God spoke to Moses, he told him: "I am the God of Abraham, Isaac and Jacob." God is a living God, so those he calls his own people must still be alive too.'

The religious teachers often argued over which part of God's law mattered most. Feelings ran high on the subject, some insisting that even the tiniest law was as important as the Ten Commandments.

One of the law teachers asked Jesus, 'Which commandment is the most important one?'

Jesus answered: ' "Love the Lord

your God with all your heart, with all your soul, and with all your mind.'' This is the greatest commandment. And the next in importance is to love others as you love yourself. These two laws belong together: keep them, and you will keep all the other laws too.'

'Tell *me* the answer!'

Sometimes Jesus turned the tables on

his questioners by asking *them* a question that they did not want to answer.

One day Jesus was telling the people the good news about God's love and forgiveness and the coming of his rule on earth. Some of the religious leaders strolled up, accompanied by leading priests and dignitaries.

'Excuse me,' they interrupted, 'will you tell us what right you have to teach like this? Who gave you permission?'

'First I will ask *you* a question,' Jesus replied. 'Answer me, and I will answer you. Do you think John the Baptist was sent from God—or did he preach and baptize in his own right?'

There was a little silence. His critics began to confer together in agitated whispers.

'What are we to answer?' they asked in desperation. 'If we tell him that John's preaching was all his own idea, the crowd will be furious. They'll stone us, most probably. They all think John was a great prophet.'

'But if we say that John's preaching was God-given, we're just as likely to be in trouble,' another one argued. 'Don't you see—Jesus will turn around and ask us why we didn't believe him and do as he said.'

In the end they replied, rather sheepishly, 'We can't answer your question.'

'Then I shall not answer yours,' Jesus told them.

Who gave God most?

Jesus and his disciples sat down for a rest near the entrance to the Court of Women. From where they sat they could see people passing the thirteen large money chests, which stood nearby. Each one had a trumpet-shaped opening to receive the gold and silver coins that would be thrown in. Many good Jewish men and women gave generous gifts towards the running costs of the temple, on top of paying their compulsory tithes (the ten per cent of their income which had to be given to God by law).

As they walked by, many richly-dressed men opened their bulging money bags with a flourish, jingled their gold coins, then threw a generous handful tinkling into the open mouth of one or other of the chests.

The disciples were very impressed. How wealthy and generous these men were and how pleased God must be with them! They scarcely noticed a shabby woman, in widow's dress, who quickly and quietly slipped two tiny coins into one of the chests before hurrying on her way. But Jesus had seen her.

'Look!' he said to the disciples. 'Did you see that woman, putting in her two coins? I can tell you that she has given more than anyone else.'

The disciples knew for a fact that this could not be true. Her two coins were the lowest value of any in circulation. How could they possibly be worth more than all those gold shekels that had gone rolling into the chests?

But before they could protest, Jesus explained.

'That widow's gift is worth most because it cost most. She gave to God all the money she had. The others may have given large amounts of gold, but they had plenty more where that came from, so it wasn't costing them much. God's arithmetic depends on how much the gift costs the giver.'

THE STORY OF
The Wicked Tenants

There was once a man who decided to plant a vineyard. He fenced in the land, built a look-out tower, and dug out a winepress. Then he let his vineyard to tenants, because he had to go on a long journey.

When it was harvest time, he sent a slave to collect his share of the grapes. But the tenants beat him and sent him back empty-handed. So the owner sent another slave but they did the same to him. Again and again the tenants ill-treated the servants he sent. Some they even killed.

Last of all he sent his son to them. 'Surely they will treat *him* with respect,' the owner said.

But when the tenants recognized who he was, they plotted together.

'Let's kill him!' they whispered. 'After all, he's the heir. Get rid of him, and the vineyard is ours!'

So they seized him, killed him, and threw his body out.

'What will the owner do next?' Jesus asked.

'He'll come himself and put those wicked tenants to death and give the vineyard to others,' some of his listeners exclaimed.

But others guessed what the story meant, and protested, 'Don't say that!'

They recognized their own religious leaders as the wicked tenants who refused to give God what they owed him. Down the centuries they had ill-treated God's messengers, the prophets. Now they were threatening to kill his own Son, Jesus.

The Jewish leaders were very angry. They knew that Jesus had told the story with them in mind and they determined to arrest him.

Towns and cities in Jesus' day were much smaller than today—and each had a protective wall around it. Country people crowded through the city gate to the market area inside, to sell their goods. The gate was the place where meetings were held, business deals made and disputes settled. Beggars would gather there—and workers waiting to be hired. At night the gate was shut.

Houses were so close-packed and streets so narrow that people could cross the city over the flat rooftops! Women met and chatted at the town well. Craftsmen and traders filled the narrow streets with varied wares—and smells! The synagogue provided a place for prayer, for studying God's law, a school and even a guest-house. Visitors and travellers stayed at the inn.

CHAPTER 21

Conspiracy to Kill

During Passover week, some of Jesus' friends in Bethany planned a special dinner for him. Martha helped to cook the food and Lazarus, her brother, was a guest too. He was the one Jesus had brought back from death.

Mary, their sister, had been longing to find some way of showing Jesus her love and thankfulness. She sensed that Jesus was feeling sad, even though he joined in the happy celebration with his friends.

While the guests were still reclining at the table, enjoying the good food, Mary slipped out. She came back carrying her most treasured possession. It was a large, sealed flask of very expensive perfume.

She came across to Jesus and, instead of letting a few drops of the precious perfume fall on his head, as a host might do to a special guest, she broke open the container so that the whole contents of the flask spilled out over Jesus' head and over his feet too.

There was a gasp of astonishment from the other guests. The pure, fragrant smell began to spread through the whole house. Mary bent and silently

wiped Jesus' feet with her long hair.

It was Judas Iscariot who broke the stunned silence.

'What a waste!' he exclaimed. 'Think how much money that flask of perfume would have fetched in the market! If Mary had given it to me to sell, I could have made a big donation to the poor.' Judas did not really care very much about poor people. But he was in charge of the funds and did well out of it himself.

Mary shrank back. But Jesus said quickly, 'Why are you upsetting Mary? Leave her alone! She has done something very beautiful for me. She has anointed my body, in advance, for my burial. You will always have the poor with you and you can meet their needs whenever you wish. But you will not always have me. I promise you that wherever in the world the good news about me is preached, the story of Mary's loving deed will also be told.'

Traitor among friends

Judas Iscariot was angry and disappointed. Jesus' reaction to the wasted perfume showed that he cared for neither money nor success.

At first Judas had been glad to be in the inner ring of Jesus' followers. After all, Jesus was the Messiah. But he wanted a Messiah who would win power and status, and bring his followers wealth and power too.

The longer Judas stayed with Jesus, the more his dreams began to fade. Jesus actually avoided power and publicity. He did not talk about his coronation, but about being arrested and put to death.

That dinner party was the last straw. Jesus did not care about wealth. Judas knew now that Jesus would never fight for his throne or win power and success for himself and his followers.

Full of bitterness and frustration, Judas left his companions and made his way up the dark narrow streets of the city to the house of the High Priest. He asked to speak to the chief priests and the temple guards. He knew that they were desperate to get Jesus in their clutches.

'What will you pay me,' he asked them, 'if I give you the information you need to find Jesus when he is on his own and take him prisoner?'

The priests exchanged surprised but gratified glances.

'Thirty silver pieces?' they suggested.

'Done!' Judas agreed.

'And payment in advance,' they added craftily, counting out the coins and placing the money bag in his eager palm. They did not want their informant

to lose his nerve or change his mind.
Money in hand would help him stick to
his bargain.

Judas walked swiftly back to join the
Twelve, planning how and when he
could betray Jesus to his enemies.

Get everything ready!

Jesus and his disciples had been in
Jerusalem nearly a week, and soon it
would be time to eat the Passover meal.

'Peter! John!' Jesus called. 'I want you
two to get the Passover meal ready for us
all.'

'Where are we going to have it?' they
asked.

'Go into the city,' Jesus told them,
'and look out for a man carrying a pitcher
of water. Follow him and he'll lead you
to the right house.'

Peter and John must have smiled. It
was like the Master to have a friend they
knew nothing about. And such an odd
friend too! Someone who sent his
manservant to fetch water, when
everyone knew that was women's work!

'When you meet the owner of the
house,' Jesus went on, 'tell him that the
Teacher says, "Where is the room we are
to use for the Passover meal?" He will
show you a large upstairs room with
table and couches all ready for dinner.
Get the food prepared there.'

Peter and John went off to do as Jesus
had said.

CHAPTER 22

The Last Passover

It had been an exciting week. The disciples would never forget the thrill of seeing their Master surrounded by cheering crowds as he rode into Jerusalem. At last he had been hailed as Messiah!

It had been breathtaking, too, when he had shown his authority in the temple court, scattering the stallholders' wares and ordering the crooked traders out of his Father's House. They forgot the darker moments, when Jesus had talked of suffering and arrest and death. Their thoughts still dwelt longingly on the day when he would be crowned king and they would proudly take their place at his side.

That evening, as they walked to the house where they were to have the Passover meal, they began to plan the future once again. But, as usual, they could not agree over who should have the key positions in Jesus' kingdom. Each one thought that *he* should be the most important.

Jesus knew only too well what they had been talking about. He turned to them and said:

'The kings of this world like to have power, and to control others, but that is not the way for you to behave. If you think that you are the greatest, the way to show it is by being willing to fetch and carry for everyone else.

'But you have stayed loyal to me through all my troubles and there is a day coming when I will give you the right to rule, just as my Father has given me that right.'

'Follow *my* example!'

When they arrived at the house, they climbed the stone steps and looked with satisfaction at the large room that Peter and John had prepared earlier that day. The table was spread, lamps were burning and everything was ready for the celebration meal.

But, as they went to take their places at table, they realized that something was missing. A basin of water and a large towel stood ready, but there was no servant at hand to help them off with

their sandals and wash their dusty feet.

Each of the disciples thought, 'It's not *my* job!' Perhaps they would have been willing to wash Jesus' feet, but to act as slave to the others was too much to ask.

Then Jesus himself stood up. He poured some water into the basin, took off his robe, with its flowing sleeves, and tied the towel around his waist. Then he went from one disciple to the other, kneeling in front of each one as he thoroughly washed and dried their dirty feet.

It was too much for Peter. 'No, Lord!' he protested. 'I'll never let you wash my feet!'

'Peter,' Jesus said gently, 'you don't understand the meaning behind what I am doing. You must let me make you clean, in every way, if you are to be part of my family.'

When Jesus had completed the circle, he said to them, 'You are right to call me your Teacher and Lord. Learn the lesson that I have been teaching you and do as I have done. Don't be self-important and expect others to wait on you. Find true happiness in following my example and looking after one another's needs.'

'One of you is a traitor'
When they had taken their places at the table, Jesus looked at them all with

great affection.

'I have so looked forward to sharing this Passover meal with you!' he said. 'This is the last time I shall eat it with you in this way.'

But, as the meal went on, a look of pain and distress crossed his face. Very sadly, he said, 'One of you sitting here is going to betray me.'

The disciples stopped eating and looked up in shock and disbelief.

'I'm telling you the truth,' Jesus insisted. 'One of you sharing this family meal will give me away to my enemies.'

First they looked at one another. Then each faced the terrible thought that he might be the guilty person. There were urgent whispers across the table, as each asked anxiously, 'It's not me, is it, Lord?'

Peter nudged John, who was reclining close to Jesus. 'Ask him which one of us it is,' he mouthed to John.

So John whispered, 'Which one of us is it, Lord?'

Quietly, so that no one else could hear, Jesus told him, 'It is the one I shall give this bread to.'

Then he dipped a piece of bread into the sauce and handed it to Judas Iscariot, as a mark of friendship.

Judas took the bread but refused the love and forgiveness that Jesus was offering. Satan, the enemy of God and all goodness, had come into his heart and hardened his resolve to sell and betray Jesus. He got up from the table abruptly and went towards the door.

'Be quick about what you are doing,' Jesus told him.

Judas was in charge of the money, so the others thought Jesus was telling him to take some money to the poor.

Only John understood the pain in Jesus' face and guessed why Judas looked hard and bitter. Judas turned on his heel and strode out into the darkness of the night.

'My body and my blood'

As they ate the Passover feast, and celebrated again God's great deliverance of his people from Egypt, the atmosphere grew solemn and quiet. The disciples sensed that something terrible but very important was soon going to happen, though they did not know what it was.

Then Jesus took some bread, broke it into pieces and handed it to his disciples to share out, as the head of the family at the Passover meal always does. But the words that he spoke had never been spoken before.

'This bread is my body,' he told them. 'Eat it.'

Next Jesus took the cup of wine, drunk at Passover in thanksgiving to God. He told them all to drink it.

'This is my blood, poured out for many,' he said. 'My blood is the seal of God's new agreement with all people.'

With wonder and awe, scarcely understanding what he could mean, the disciples took the bread and wine from their Master's hands and ate and drank.

'Do this in memory of me,' Jesus told them.

'We'll never leave you!'

Together they sang the Passover hymn:

'Give thanks to God, for he is good,
His love goes on for ever.'

Then they talked comfortably, as friends do, lingering together in the room, delaying the moment when they would leave. They felt very close to each other and to Jesus, their Master.

As if he guessed their feelings he said, 'I am the vine and you are all like branches that grow from me. That's how close we are. If you want your lives to produce love and patience and kindness, as the vine's branches produce grapes, you must stay close to me and obey me. Then my life will flow through you, making you strong and fruitful for me.

'I have so much more to explain to you,' Jesus went on, 'and so little time to talk. In a little while you won't see me any more, but a little while afterwards, you will see me again.'

'What *does* he mean?' they asked one another, puzzled. 'We don't understand what he's talking about.'

'Listen,' Jesus went on, 'I am going to leave you and you will be sad. But later on your sadness will turn to happiness. Very soon now, you are all going to desert me. You will scatter in all directions and I shall be left alone. But I'm never really alone, because my Father is always with me.'

'I'll never leave you!' Peter exclaimed confidently. 'The others may, but I won't!'

'We won't desert you, either!' the others insisted.

Jesus turned to Peter and said sadly, 'Tonight, before cockcrow, you will say three times over that you do not know me.'

'I'll never say that!' Peter protested. 'Even if it means dying with you!' The others said the same.

'Trust me!'

The disciples felt anxious and disturbed. Although they could not understand half of what Jesus was saying, they knew he was warning them of bad times ahead. They left the warmth and light of the room with a strong sense of foreboding and stepped into the chill of the spring night. Then they began the steep descent to the valley.

Jesus looked at their downcast faces with love and concern.

'Don't be worried!' he told them. 'Put your trust in God, and trust me too. There are many rooms in my Father's house. I am going away so that I can get a home ready for you. Then I will come and fetch you to be with me for ever. You know the way to the place where I am going.'

'We don't even know where you are going,' Thomas complained, 'so how can we know the way to get there?'

'I am the way to God, Thomas,' Jesus explained. 'No one goes to the Father, except through me. But even though I am going away, you won't be left all alone. I shall ask the Father to send you another Helper—the Spirit of God. He will help you to know the truth and to remember all the things I have told you. He will never leave you on your own.

'Peace is my parting gift to you—my peace. I have tried to warn you about what is going to happen, so that your faith won't be shattered when the time comes. This is the hour when Satan's evil power is at large. But he has no power over me. My Father is in control. You *will* have trouble in this world. But be brave! I have conquered the world!'

In Jesus' day, crowds of visitors flocked to Jerusalem every Spring to celebrate Passover—the festival that looks back to the time when God delivered his people from slavery in Egypt. Then, a lamb had been killed for each Jewish family, and death had 'passed over' their homes, sparing their lives. So at Passover each family group sacrificed a lamb at the temple before roasting and eating it, with other special foods. During the meal, the youngest child asked what this meant, and the father told the story.

Passover begins the Festival of Unleavened Bread, when, for a whole week, no 'leaven' (yeast) may be used in baking. Before the festival begins, the home is 'spring-cleaned', and children join the search for any leavened dough.

Preparations begin at home: leavened dough must be found and thrown away.

Pilgrims from far and wide flock to Jerusalem for Passover.

A lamb is taken to the temple to be killed by the priest.

At home, the lamb for the Passover meal is roasted, and special food prepared.

The family gathers for the meal. 'What does this mean?' asks the youngest child—and father explains.

CHAPTER 23

In the Dark of the Night

Jesus and the eleven disciples reached the Kidron Valley, then made their way, as they had planned, to the olive grove of Gethsemane. The owner always welcomed Jesus and his followers to enjoy its coolness and quiet at night.

They walked for a while over the bare, stony ground, under the silver-green leaves and gnarled branches of the olive-trees. Then Jesus stopped.

'Sit here and rest,' he told his disciples. 'I'm going further on to pray.'

He beckoned to Peter and James and John to follow him, and strode purposefully into thicker shade, where the bright moon shone less clearly.

'Please keep me company,' he told the three friends, his voice full of sadness and distress. 'I feel crushed and broken by grief.'

They looked at his face, stricken with pain, wondering what he could mean. As they watched, feeling powerless to help, Jesus went a little further, then threw himself down on the ground and began to pray out loud in great distress.

'My Father,' they heard him say, 'please—if it is possible—take this terrible cup of suffering away from me!' Then, in calmer tones, he pleaded, 'But don't give me what *I* want. Let *your* plan for me be done.'

Peter and James and John were tired out as well as being confused and upset.

As they waited for Jesus to come back to them, they fell fast asleep.

It seemed only a moment later that they heard the Master's voice, close by them.

'Couldn't you keep watch with me even for an hour?' he asked, in disappointment. 'You need to pray, too, and be on your guard, so that you don't fail when you are tested.'

They felt bitterly ashamed that they had let their best friend down when he needed them most. But when he went away a second and a third time to pray, they could not keep their eyes open. They dozed off again, overcome with tiredness and grief.

The third time Jesus came back, he said, 'Get up! The time has come. Let's go.'

Arrest in the garden

As they rejoined the others, Jesus said, 'Look! Here comes the one who has betrayed me!'

In the distance, steadily coming closer, they could make out a bobbing line of torches. Soon they were able to distinguish the forms of soldiers, part of the armed guard belonging to the High Priest. They were accompanied by rough-looking men carrying clubs and makeshift weapons.

At the head of the column was a familiar figure. Judas stepped out of the shadows.

'Hello, Teacher!' he said, and greeted Jesus with a respectful kiss.

That was the pre-arranged signal. Now the soldiers knew which man to arrest.

'Are you betraying me with a kiss?' Jesus asked him sadly.

Then he turned to the waiting guard.

'Who is it you want?' he asked them.

'Jesus of Nazareth,' they replied.

'I am the one you want,' Jesus confirmed, 'so let these others go free. But why have you come to arrest me by force, as if I am a dangerous criminal? You could have taken me at any time during the day, while I was sitting teaching in the temple court.'

With a show of force, the soldiers stepped forward and surrounded Jesus, holding him tightly.

Peter could contain himself no longer. He rushed forward, brandishing a sword, and slashed through the air

160

uncertainly, slicing off the ear of one of the guards near to Jesus.

'That's enough, Peter!' Jesus said. 'Put your sword away. Don't you know that if I wanted to escape I could call to my Father? He would send huge armies of angels to rescue me. But all that is happening now is part of God's plan.'

Then Jesus gently touched the man's ear, and healed him.

At that moment the truth dawned on the disciples. Jesus was not going to slip away as he had done at other times when an angry mob had tried to kill him. He was going meekly with these men, to face almost certain death.

Gripped by panic, despair and bewilderment, they took to their heels and ran off as fast as they could go.

Trial Time

The armed guards tied Jesus up and led him away, across the Kidron Valley, and up into the city, to the house of Annas. He had once been the High Priest, but his son-in-law, Caiaphas, now held the post. He was there too, and began to cross-question Jesus about the things that he had taught the people.

'My teaching has never been secret,' Jesus told him. 'Anyone listening in the crowd could tell you what I said.'

One of the guards slapped Jesus' face.

'How dare you talk to the High Priest like that?' he demanded angrily.

Then, still tied up, Jesus was taken to Caiaphas' house. Other members of the seventy-strong Sanhedrin Council had been hurriedly sent for.

For hour after hour they questioned Jesus, trying to force him to say

something that they could use as proof that he had committed a crime. They produced witnesses, who made up false stories about Jesus, but none of them told the same tale, so their evidence could not be used.

Peter fails the test

After the first blind panic, which had made them run from Gethsemane with the other disciples, Peter and John came to their senses. They retraced their steps in time to see the guards, with their prisoner, climbing the steep road to the city.

When Jesus was taken to the High Priest's house, John suggested that they

should go there too. He knew some of the members of the household, so he would be allowed to go inside the courtyard.

He left Peter at the entrance, then asked the girl at the gate if he could bring his friend in too.

As soon as she saw Peter, she said, 'Here, you're another follower of that man, aren't you?' and she pointed towards the room, off the courtyard, where Jesus stood facing his accusers.

Panic struck Peter again.

'No I am not!' he almost shouted.

It was a cold evening, and the servants had lighted a brazier in the middle of the courtyard. Peter joined the others sitting around it, but he felt even more scared when he recognized some of the men who had been in the party that arrested Jesus.

He knew that they were staring hard at him. Then one of them said, 'You're from Galilee by the way you speak. You're one of his lot.' He jerked his head towards the room where Jesus stood.

'No, I'm not! I'll swear I'm not!' Peter protested, scarcely daring to look up.

But a little later another man, who had been in Gethsemane, and was a relative of the slave whose ear Peter had cut off, came across and said, 'I saw you in the olive grove with Jesus. I'm certain you were there!'

'I never knew the man!' he shouted. 'I swear I am telling the truth—may God punish me if I am not!'

At that very moment a cockerel crowed. Jesus' words came rushing back to Peter, burning in his memory. He looked across to where his Master stood. Jesus turned and looked at him. Torn with grief and remorse, Peter rushed from the courtyard, weeping bitterly.

Verdict—guilty!

All night long the ordeal continued. Every attempt to prove Jesus guilty of wrongdoing failed utterly. At last, desperate to convict him, the High Priest asked point blank, 'Are you the Messiah, the Son of Almighty God?'

Now, at last, questioned under oath, Jesus declared, 'I am. And the day is coming when you will see the Son of man seated at God's right hand and coming with the clouds of heaven!'

There was a gasp of horror. The High Priest stood up, ripping his ceremonial robe as a sign of his outrage and distress.

'We need no more evidence!' he declared to the assembled Council. 'You have heard his wicked words, claiming to be God. What is your verdict?'

'He is guilty and he must die!' they shouted angrily.

Some of them began to spit at him. Then the guards took charge of Jesus. For the rest of that night, they blindfolded, teased and tormented him, and struck him with brutal force.

When morning came, the Sanhedrin met officially to confirm the death penalty and to plan how best to persuade the Roman Governor to confirm and carry out the sentence they had passed.

A traitor's end

When Judas heard that the Jewish court had condemned Jesus to death, he was filled with remorse. Perhaps he had expected Jesus to save himself by some last-minute miracle. Perhaps it was only now, when Jesus faced death, that the awfulness of what he had done dawned upon Judas.

He rushed through the temple courts until he reached the area reserved for priests.

'I'm guilty! I have betrayed an innocent man!' he shouted wildly. 'Take your money back!'

'That's your affair,' they replied coolly. 'It's nothing to do with us.'

In desperation, Judas hurled the thirty silver coins into the court and rushed out of the temple precincts.

Then he hanged himself.

Trial by the Romans

Pilate, the Roman Governor, always came to Jerusalem for Passover week, to keep a close watch on proceedings. When large crowds of people in holiday mood are packed together, feelings run high and trouble is likely to flare up.

Early that Friday morning, the Jewish leaders took Jesus, their condemned prisoner, to Pilate. They knew that, in order to persuade Pilate to condemn Jesus to death, they must accuse him of crimes against Rome. Pilate would not care how many Jewish laws Jesus was supposed to have broken.

'This prisoner is guilty of misleading the common people,' they told him. 'He tells them to stop paying their taxes to the Emperor and says that he is a king.'

Pilate took Jesus inside for questioning, while the Jewish leaders waited.

'Are you really a king?' he asked him.

'My kingdom does not belong to this world,' Jesus said, 'or else my subjects would fight to save me from being handed over to my enemies. I came into this world in order to speak about the truth.'

'What is truth?' Pilate asked. He had learned to do what caused least trouble, not what was right or true. But he was sure that Jesus was innocent and that the leaders had accused him because they were jealous of him.

So Pilate went out to the members of the Council and said, 'This man is wholly innocent. He has done nothing to deserve death.'

But they insisted: 'If you don't silence him, there will be a riot.'

They knew that Pilate would be in serious trouble with the Roman Emperor if fighting broke out. He must avoid that at all costs.

When Pilate discovered that Jesus came from Galilee, he tried to shift the responsibility by sending him to Herod, who ruled that province under Rome. Herod, too, was in Jerusalem for Passover. He had heard a lot about Jesus and was delighted at the prospect of seeing him in person. He hoped he might see him perform one of his famous miracles.

But when Jesus stood as a prisoner before Herod, he would not speak one word to him or satisfy his idle curiosity. He remembered Herod's hardness in the face of John's preaching.

Herod and his soldiers ill-treated Jesus and made fun of him. Then they sent him back to Pilate.

By this time, a crowd had collected beneath the balcony of the palace. When they saw Jesus, tied up, and bleeding from the knocks and cuffs he had received, they began to chant: 'Crucify! Crucify!', over and over again.

Pilate still hoped to save Jesus' life.

'You know I set one prisoner free at Passover,' he told the crowds. 'This year I'll set Jesus free.'

But the fickle crowd, led on by the religious leaders, shouted, 'Kill him! Kill him! Set Barabbas free!'

Barabbas was in prison for starting a riot, as well as for murder.

Pilate was worried. The roar of the mob grew louder. He saw their clenched fists and heard their stamping feet. He must keep the situation under control. He was unpopular enough already. He

must not make the people angry, or risk being reported to Rome. Jesus and the truth must take second place.

He called for a basin of water, washed his hands for everyone to see, then announced, 'I wash my hands of this whole affair. This man's death is your responsibility. I will release Barabbas and order the execution of the prisoner, Jesus.'

CHAPTER 25

The Way of the Cross

Pilate did as he had promised. He ordered that Barabbas should be released and that Jesus should be whipped, then handed over to the Roman execution squad to be crucified.

Jesus was escorted down into the courtyard where the off-duty soldiers joined the guards on duty in teasing and tormenting their prisoner. Jesus' back was already raw and bleeding from the vicious strokes of the metal-tipped whip.

They had heard that Jesus was accused of trying to make himself king. So they made a game out of dressing him up in a red robe, and pretending to bow and scrape to him. One of the soldiers ripped off some thorn branches, twisted them into a rough circle, then jammed the imitation crown hard on to Jesus' head, so that the sharp thorns pierced the skin. Then they beat him over the head and spat at him.

There were two other prisoners lined up, waiting to be escorted to Golgotha for crucifixion. Golgotha means 'skull place', a suitable name for the site, outside the city walls, where executions were carried out.

Soon the sad little procession set off, the prisoners struggling to keep up with the soldiers' brisk march. Each one had to carry the heavy cross beam to which his arms would be nailed when his body was hoisted on to the upright post.

Although many of the ordinary people had joined in the shouts of 'crucify', and were going along to watch the fun, not everyone in the crowd was hard-hearted. Some of the women who jostled alongside the prisoners and their escorts were crying as they saw Jesus, bruised and bleeding from his injuries. They remembered the way he had cared for the sick and fed the hungry.

But Jesus told them, 'Don't cry for me! Weep for yourselves and your children. Terrible times are coming for this city!'

Jesus was weak from loss of blood and the effects of the long night's interrogation. Soon he could no longer stagger along under the heavy weight of his cross. So the centurion stopped a passer-by called Simon, a visitor from Cyrene in North Africa. He tapped him on the shoulder with the flat of his spear, and ordered him to carry Jesus' cross for him. Simon had to obey this command from a Roman officer, so he shouldered the cross beam and took his place in the procession.

Death by crucifixion

Crucifixion was a common death for runaway slaves and rebels against Rome and the execution squads were used to carrying it out. When they arrived at Golgotha, the crowd watched while the Roman soldiers went through the familiar routine.

First they handed Jesus a drink of wine. It helped to deaden pain, and was supplied by a group of kind women. But Jesus would not drink it. Then they nailed Jesus on to the middle cross, crucifying the other two victims on

either side of him.

The criminal's name and crime had to be written over his cross. Pilate himself ordered the wording above Jesus' cross:

'Jesus of Nazareth, the King of the Jews.'

The Jewish leaders were indignant.

'Don't put "The King of the Jews",' they begged Pilate. 'Put, "This man said, 'I am the King of the Jews.'"' But Pilate refused to listen.

'What I have written stays as it is,' he told them, with grim satisfaction at their dismay.

There was no more, now, for the execution squad to do but keep watch while the prisoners died their lingering and agonizing death. They would be on duty many hours—even days. They shared out the prisoners' clothes, which were theirs by right, tossing up to see who should have the best. Then they sat down to wait. But they could not take their eyes off the one who hung on the cross in the middle.

A mixed crowd stood around, watching the dying men with horror and fascination. The priests and leaders who had brought about Jesus' death were there and they went on taunting and teasing him.

'Aren't you supposed to be God's Son? Then prove it by coming down from the cross!' one of them shouted.

'Yes,' another one joined in. 'If God is so pleased with you, why doesn't he rescue you?'

The two criminals cursed and groaned, but Jesus prayed for those who were putting him to death.

'Father, forgive them, they don't know what they are doing,' he said.

'Remember me, Jesus!'

One of the criminals, hanging alongside Jesus, began to join in the insults and abuse.

'If you say that you're Messiah, why don't you save yourself—and us too?' he asked.

But his mate turned on him.

'How do you dare to talk like that?' he asked. 'We are all getting the same punishment, but at least we deserve what's coming to us. This man hasn't done anything wrong.' Then, painfully, he turned towards Jesus.

'Remember me, Jesus,' he murmured, 'on the day when you come as King!'

'I promise you,' Jesus told him, 'that you will be in Paradise with me this very day!'

'It's finished!'

Some of Jesus' close friends and relatives stood around his cross too. They could scarcely bear to see him in such pain, but they wanted to be near him. All they could hope was to give him some comfort by staying close. Jesus looked down at the sad figure of his mother. He longed to take care of her. Then he saw John, his special disciple and friend, close by.

'Here is your son,' he told his mother. Then to John he said, 'There is your mother.'

That very day, John took Mary to his own home and looked after her.

At noon, after three hours had passed, when the sun was reaching its highest point and the heat was steadily increasing, a strange and frightening darkness fell. Jesus' agony was hidden from the crowd, but his voice could be heard in a terrible cry.

'My God,' he called out, 'why did you forsake me?'

Later they heard him repeat the prayer that Mary had taught him to say, like all Jewish boys, every morning and night, 'Father, into your hands I commit myself.'

Then in a loud voice he cried out, 'It is finished!'

His head sank forward and he gave his life into God's keeping.

The Roman centurion in charge had witnessed many crucifixions. But, as he looked at this prisoner, he knew that Jesus was unlike any other victim he had executed. He was filled with awe and wonder.

'This man really was the Son of God!' he confessed.

The Silent Sabbath

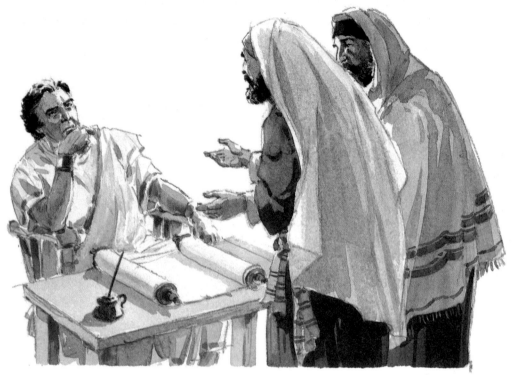

It was a Friday when Jesus was crucified and, as the day drew on, the Jewish leaders became concerned. The three men must be dead and removed from their crosses before sunset. That was when the Sabbath would begin and, by Jewish law, even a criminal's body must be buried before the Sabbath day, especially at Passover time.

They decided to ask Pilate if the victims' legs could be broken, so that they would die more quickly. Pilate agreed and the Roman centurion in charge of the execution was given the order.

The soldiers broke the legs of the two criminals, but when they examined Jesus they confirmed the fact that he was already dead.

Jesus' friends were watching from a little distance now, sad that none of them could afford to give their Master a proper burial. They did not want him to be put in a mass grave.

But Jesus had friends and followers among the wealthy citizens of Jerusalem. One of them, Joseph, was a member of the Sanhedrin. He had not voted for Jesus' death, like most of the others, but he had kept silent, afraid to admit openly that he was a follower of Jesus.

Now he plucked up courage to go to Pilate. He begged to have Jesus' body in order to give it proper burial, and Pilate gave his permission.

Nicodemus, another religious leader, helped Joseph. He had once visited

Jesus under cover of darkness and talked for a long time with him. Together they took the body off the cross, washed it, and gently wrapped it in linen, lined with myrrh and other fragrant spices used to anoint the dead. Then they wrapped a linen cloth around his head.

Near to the skull-like rock of Golgotha, where Jesus had been crucified, there was a tomb, recently dug out of solid rock, which Joseph had prepared for his own burial. They had to work quickly, for time was short. The sun was setting and the Sabbath would soon begin: no work must be done after that.

The two men carried their precious burden and carefully laid it on a rocky ledge, carved from the wall inside the tomb. Then they came outside into the garden, and rolled a huge boulder over the entrance, to keep the body safe from prowling animals.

Jesus' enemies were taking no chances. They remembered that Jesus had spoken about rising from death. Suppose his followers decided to spirit the body away under cover of darkness, and then make out that their leader had come to life again?

'Send some soldiers to guard the tomb,' Pilate said, when they told him their fears. 'Make it as secure as you like.'

So they fixed a seal to the stone that blocked the mouth of the tomb. No one could tamper with it now without being discovered. Then they left a guard on duty.

Silent watchers
While Joseph and Nicodemus were busy about their task, the women disciples watched them. They had stayed close to Jesus while he hung on the cross. One of

them was Mary, from Magdala, a
lakeside town in Galilee. She had been a
sick, tormented woman until the day
when Jesus healed and rescued her, and
she had been his devoted follower ever
since. Another disciple, also called
Mary, went with her, following the two
men as they placed Jesus' body inside
the tomb.

They looked inside, to see just where
the body was lying, then, when the stone
had been rolled into place, blocking the
entrance, they sat quietly outside for a
while, mourning their lost Master.

They longed to be able to show their
love and respect for Jesus by adding
their gift of spices and perfumes to
anoint his body. But sunset was near and
no work must be done until sunset the
next day. They must wait patiently for
the sad slow hours to pass, until the
Sabbath was over.

The climate is hot in Palestine: so funerals took place the day someone died, at the time of Jesus. The body was washed and tightly wrapped in long strips of linen cloth, packed with spices. Then it was carried on a rough wickerwork stretcher to the burial place—often a cave on the hillside, with ledges to take the bodies. The entrance was filled with a large stone, so that animals could not get in.

Later, the bones might be put in a small stone box, to save space.

Relatives and friends tore their clothes to show their grief, and hired mourners to wail and play the flute. No food could be prepared in the dead person's house for a week, and those who could stopped work to mourn together.

Inside the tomb

CHAPTER 27

The First Day of the Week

peering in the dim light at the stone ledge where Joseph and Nicodemus had placed the body of their Master. To their horror, the body had gone.

They stood still for a moment, shocked and bewildered, then ran as fast as they could to find Peter and John.

'Come quick!' they begged. 'Someone has stolen his body!' The two friends set off together, but John ran faster and reached the tomb first. Peter, coming up behind, burst straight into the burial chamber. It was just as the women had said. He gazed at the empty linen grave

Very early on Sunday morning, before it was really light, the two Marys set off for Jesus' tomb, taking perfume and precious spices to put on his body.

In the half-light they were surprised to see that the huge stone, which had blocked the entrance, had been rolled away. Bravely, they ventured inside, cloths, still lying in place and, a little apart, the cloth that had been wrapped around Jesus' head.

John tiptoed up behind him and, as he gazed, Jesus' words about rising from death came back to his mind. A glimmer of understanding began to light up his dark, sad thoughts. But he said nothing, and he and Peter walked thoughtfully home.

These four were not the only visitors to the tomb that Sunday morning. Afterwards, when they tried to piece together all that had happened, they could never quite agree about the details or decide in which order the amazing events of that day took place.

Some of those early visitors had seen bright, shining angels. Some said there were two of them, sitting on the ledge where Jesus' body had been put. Others were sure they had seen just one shining messenger, seated on the huge stone that had been rolled away. But they all remembered what the heavenly messengers had said.

'Why are you looking in a tomb for someone who is alive? Jesus is not here, he has risen from death, just as he promised he would!'

Earthquake at dawn

At dawn that day the soldiers guarding the tomb on the orders of the religious leaders had been scared out of their wits. First an earthquake shook the ground beneath their feet. Then a dazzling figure had swooped down, breaking the seal on the huge stone and hurling it away from the entrance.

As soon as their legs stopped trembling, the terrified soldiers hurried to report to the priests.

'Don't breathe a word of this to anyone else,' the priests told them. 'We will pay you well to say that his disciples stole his body in the night, when you had fallen asleep on watch. We'll see that you don't get into trouble with the Roman Governor.'

The frightened soldiers did as they were told.

'Are you the gardener?'

When Peter and John left, Mary Magdalene stayed on in the garden, close the garden, close to the tomb. She cried as she looked once more into the dark recess. But now, in the dim light, she could make out two white-clothed figures.

'Why are you crying?' one of them asked her.

'Because they have taken my Lord's body away, and I don't know where it is,' Mary answered, tearfully.

As she turned she saw another figure, standing behind her in the garden. He asked the same question.

'Why are you crying? Who are you looking for?'

Perhaps he was the gardener, Mary thought. With a small ray of hope, she asked, 'Are you the person who moved the body from the tomb? If so, please tell me where it is, so that I can fetch it back.'

'Mary!' the stranger said, in a voice she knew so well.

She wheeled around to face him.

'Master!' she exclaimed, clutching hold of him.

'Don't keep me now,' Jesus said gently, 'for I am on my way to my Father. Go and tell the others that I am going to my Father, who is your Father too—to my God and your God.'

Messiah, was now dead and buried. Some of the women were repeating wild tales that they had seen a vision of angels who said that Jesus was alive. But who could believe that? They felt certain now that their hopes and happiness were at an end.

Someone else on the same road caught up with them and matched his steps with theirs. But they took scarcely any notice of him until he spoke.

'You are looking very miserable,' he remarked. 'What's the matter? What are you talking about?'

Surely he must know what had been happening in Jerusalem! But it was a relief to pour out their troubles to a sympathetic listener and soon they had told him the whole sad story.

'So Jesus, our Master, is dead, and he can't have been the promised Messiah after all,' they concluded miserably.

But the stranger exclaimed, 'How can you be so foolish? Haven't you read the Scriptures? Don't you understand what the prophets foretold about the Messiah?'

Then he began to explain to them one Scripture passage after another. Some verses, like those by Isaiah, told of the perfect Servant, sent by God, who would suffer and die for his people's sins. This Messiah was like a lamb, sacrificed on behalf of the people. Like the Passover lamb, his death would be the means of deliverance and freedom.

The two listened spellbound. Their teachers had never explained the Scriptures as this man did. Before they knew it, they had arrived at their own door.

The sun was setting. Soon it would be dark. But the stranger seemed as if he was going further.

'Look—it's nearly night time,' they

Fellow travellers

Cleopas and his companion trudged along the road from Jerusalem to their own village of Emmaus, about eight miles away. They were plunged in despair. They had been followers of Jesus too and, as they walked, they talked over the happenings of the last terrible days.

They were heartbroken that Jesus, the one they loved and believed to be the

said. 'Why not come in and have supper with us?'

He readily agreed, and soon the table was spread for a simple meal.

As if it were the most natural thing in the world, their visitor moved to the host's place. He gave thanks to God for the food and began to share it out. Then, in a flash, they recognized him.

'Jesus! Master!' they exclaimed. But he had gone.

Talking and laughing excitedly, they set off at once, going back to Jerusalem with the wonderful news that Jesus was alive.

Jesus *is* alive!

Breathlessly, the two disciples from Emmaus pushed open the door of the upstairs room where the other disciples were sitting together. But before they could utter a word, they were met by a chorus of excited voices, 'The Lord is risen! Peter has seen him!'

'We've seen him too!' the new arrivals exclaimed and began to describe their wonderful walk to Emmaus.

While they were still telling their story, Jesus himself appeared in the room. At first they were all terrified. They thought that they were seeing a ghost.

But Jesus gave a big smile and held out his hands.

'Look!' he said. 'I'm real! Ghosts don't have flesh or bones as I have. Is there anything to eat?'

And as they watched, all eyes upon him, he ate the cooked fish they gave him.

'Have you forgotten all the things I taught you?' he asked. 'My death was not a mistake. The prophets declared that the Messiah would suffer and die, to

179

bring forgiveness and new life for everyone. They said that he would rise to life, as I have done. Now the good news can be spread far and wide. People everywhere can turn back to God and receive forgiveness for their sins.'

'Give me proof!'

When Jesus appeared to his followers that Sunday evening, Thomas, one of the twelve disciples, was not there. As soon as the others saw him again they told him excitedly, 'Jesus is alive! We've seen him with our own eyes!'

'I must see him for myself before I believe that,' Thomas replied. 'I need proper proof that you aren't imagining the whole thing. When I can touch his hands and side and feel the holes the nails made, I'll believe—but not before.'

The next Sunday the disciples were together in the same upstairs room, and this time Thomas was with them.

Suddenly, Jesus came to them again.

'Peace to you all,' he said. Then he looked straight at Thomas.

'Put your finger here,' he said, 'and touch my hands. Stretch your hand out and feel my side. Stop doubting and believe!'

Thomas did not need to touch the scars or to look for proof any more. He fell to his knees in front of Jesus.

'My Lord and my God!' he exclaimed.

'Thomas,' Jesus said gently, 'you believe because you have seen with your own eyes. There will be a special blessing for all those who believe, without ever having seen me.'

CHAPTER 28

New Mission

All Jesus' friends and disciples had seen him now. They knew for certain that he was alive again. But some of the first excitement had died down by the time Peter and his friends left Jerusalem and went home to Galilee.

They knew that the old days had gone for ever, but they still did not know what the future held. Meanwhile Peter, for one, had a family to feed.

'I'm going fishing,' he told the others, one evening.

'We'll come too,' they agreed. So Peter, James and John, with four others, climbed into Peter's boat. Soon they were off, rowing across the darkening waters of the lake.

All night long they fished. Again and again they cast the net over the side of the boat, only to haul it in empty. When the first thin light of dawn began to turn the black waters to silver, they had caught nothing. Wearily they began to row back towards the shore.

As they came nearer, they could make out a figure, outlined by the light of the sun. He cupped his hands and hailed them, and his voice carried clearly across the water:

'Have you caught anything, lads?' he called.

'Not a thing!' they shouted back.

'Then throw the net over the right side of the boat and you will,' he told them.

For some reason it seemed natural to do as the stranger said. And no sooner had they cast the net into the water than a shoal of wriggling fish began to swarm into it. In a few moments it was too full and heavy to drag back on board.

'You know who it is?' John whispered excitedly to Peter. 'It's the Lord!'

Peter's mind flashed back to the day when he first decided to follow Jesus. Jesus had borrowed his boat to preach from, then, afterwards, told Peter to cast his net into the sea. What an enormous catch of fish he had landed that day! And how sinful and unworthy of Jesus he had felt!

It was the same now. He had failed his Master just when he needed him most. Yet Jesus was here, loving him and meeting his needs as he had always done.

In one swift movement Peter jumped into the water, plunging towards the shore. He left the others to drag the net and the boat up the beach.

He saw a charcoal fire glowing hot, on a pile of large stones. There was a wonderful smell of fish grilling on the

embers and fresh, warm bread lay ready.

'Bring some of the fish you have caught,' Jesus told them and Peter rushed back again to bring the net on shore. One of them counted the fish and found that there were one hundred and fifty-three. But the net did not tear, even though it was so full.

'Come and have something to eat!' Jesus said. None of them asked who he was. They all knew now.

Then, when they had sat down, Jesus brought a delicious breakfast of fish and bread to each one in turn.

'Do you love me?'

When breakfast was over and everyone was warm and full, Jesus walked alone with Peter, along the water's edge. They were silent for a while, then Jesus asked, 'Peter, do you love me more than

anything or anyone else?'

'Yes, Lord,' Peter said fervently. 'You know I do.'

'Then take care of my sheep,' Jesus told him.

Twice more Jesus asked, 'Do you love me, Peter?' and twice more Peter told Jesus that he loved him. Each time, Jesus gave Peter his new task—to look after Jesus' flock of followers.

At first Peter was sad to think that Jesus doubted him and needed to ask so many times if he loved him. Then he felt glad that Jesus had given him three chances to declare his love, as if to wipe out those three times he had denied knowing his Master. He was excited and grateful. Although he had let his Master down so badly, Jesus was ready to trust Peter and let him work for him again.

Peter wondered what plans Jesus had

in store for the other disciples. He saw John close behind and asked, 'What about John, Lord? What will happen to him?'

'That is not your business, Peter,' Jesus replied. 'Just see to it that *you* follow me!'

The whole wide world

For about six weeks, Jesus kept appearing at different times to his disciples. He taught them many things that they had not been able to understand before his death and resurrection.

They never knew quite when he would come or go. Doors and locks were no barrier to him. But although his body was different, he was real, more real than ever, and their fears and doubts were laid to rest.

When the Jewish Festival of Pentecost was near, the disciples went back to Jerusalem. Jesus met them and took them along the familiar route out of the city and up the steep path to the Mount of Olives.

Their hopes rose again. Perhaps now was the time for Jesus to be crowned King. This was the place where the prophet had said that Messiah would stand.

'Will you be crowned King now?' they asked.

But Jesus replied, 'God will decide when that time comes. It is not for you to know. I have other work for you to do. I am going to send you into the whole wide world to make others my disciples too. Everyone who turns back to God will find forgiveness and new life.

'God has given me charge over everything in heaven and on earth, and I promise to be with you to the very end. My Holy Spirit will soon come, and he will never leave you. Wait for him here in Jerusalem. You will need his help and power as you go to tell the good news far and wide.'

The disciples gazed at Jesus, scarcely able to take in what he was saying. Then he stretched out his hands to bless them and, as they watched, he went from their sight.

They knew now that they would not see him again. They looked upwards, as he went, and saw the cloud of God's presence, as they had done when Jesus talked with Moses and Elijah on the mountain-top. Then their dazzled eyes came to rest on two bright beings standing beside them.

'Why are you staring up into the sky?' the shining ones asked. 'Jesus will come back again one day, in the same way that you saw him go.'

Although Jesus had gone away, home to his Father, they did not feel sad. There was a spring in their step as they hurried down the hill and back to their meeting-place in Jerusalem.

They had work to do for Jesus. Soon, when his Spirit came to help them, they would tell the whole world the good news about their Master and King.

All the close friends of Jesus stayed together in Jerusalem, as Jesus had told them to. They spent their time praying, and praising God in the temple, as they waited for the promised Holy Spirit to arrive.

Postscript

What happened next?

Matthew, Mark and John finish their Gospels without telling us the end of the story of Jesus which they began. But we *do* know what happened next, thanks to Luke. He wrote a sequel, continuing where he had left off. His second book is called *The Acts of the Apostles* and comes after the Gospel of John in the New Testament.

Luke tells us that when Jesus returned to his Father, God, the apostles, along with other men and women disciples, waited together at Jerusalem as he had told them to do. It was not long before Jesus kept his promise and sent his Holy Spirit to them. Because he is spirit, he did not come in the same way Jesus did, but the disciples saw outward signs of his arrival—flashing fire and the noise of a tremendous wind. He came to each one of them in turn and they knew in that moment that Jesus was with them again, never to go away, closer than ever before.

It was the Holy Spirit who made Peter brave enough to preach to the crowds who had gathered, telling his startled listeners that Jesus, the one they had crucified, was alive again. When he explained that they had shouted for God's Messiah to be put to death, they were full of remorse. Thousands came forward to confess their sin, be baptized and become Jesus' followers. Peter told them that now they too would have the Holy Spirit within them.

That day the new Christian church was born. It soon grew in strength and numbers, in spite of all that the religious leaders could do. They arrested the apostles and threw them into prison but they could not stop them or the other Christians spreading the good news about Jesus. The apostles healed many people, in Jesus' name, as he had done.

At first only Jewish men and women became Christians. But God made it clear to Peter and the other apostles that he wanted to bring people of every nation into his family.

One person in particular, a young man called Saul, took the gospel to Gentiles. He had been a leading Pharisee who tried his best to stamp out the young church. But one day he had a vision of Jesus which turned him from an enemy into one of Jesus' staunchest followers. Saul was also a Roman citizen, and he set off on preaching expeditions all over the Roman Empire, founding new young churches in many cities. Using his Gentile name of Paul, he wrote letters to help the new Christians understand their faith and put it into practice. These letters, or epistles, are part of the New Testament writings too.

Other Christians, ordinary travellers or traders, carried the good news of the gospel wherever they went, passing it on to those they met on the way or in the market-place.

Sooner or later, by one means or another, and often at great cost, the gospel reached the lands where we live today.

The story of Jesus does not have an ending. Because he is alive today, Jesus still meets the needs of all kinds of people. He forgives them and gives peace as well as meaning to life. His Spirit still comes into the lives of those who trust and love him.

One day Jesus will keep his promise to return to our world. Then everything that is bad and evil will be gone for ever, and he will make the world new. Jesus will rule in peace and justice. The story will go on for ever.

List of Special Words, with their Meanings

Angels

Angels are God's messengers and live in God's world. They sometimes appeared with a special message from God but usually they cannot be seen, although they are always around us to protect and help. No one knows what angels look like, but they share the brightness of God's world and the sight of them brings awe and fear.

Apostle

Apostle means 'sent one'. Jesus called his twelve disciples 'apostles' because he was sending them out to preach the good news.

Coinage

In Jesus' day, they used a mixture of Roman, Greek and Jewish coins. The temple tax could be paid only in Jewish coins, so money-changers set up their stalls in the temple courtyard. They often cheated on the exchange rate.

Disciples

A disciple is someone who follows and learns from his teacher. John the Baptist had disciples and Jesus had many—men and women—in addition to the twelve apostles who are often referred to as 'the disciples'.

Disease

There were many sick people in Jesus' day and not many known cures for illness. Eye and skin diseases were very common. Evil spirits were thought to cause certain diseases. The priest was trained to recognize skin diseases and to pronounce a person cured. Olive oil and wine were used to clean and heal wounds. Balsam from the trees in Jericho was famous for its soothing powers.

Gentiles

The word means 'nation' and was used by Jewish people to refer to members of every nation other than their own. Most religious Jews thought that, because the Jews were God's special people, Gentiles had no place in God's loving plans.

Food

Poor people ate mostly barley or lentil porridge, with perhaps some salted fish for Sabbath. Meat was eaten only on feast days. Richer people might have titbits of mutton with their rice or barley or wheat. (Fat tails of sheep were a delicacy!) There were onions and leeks and cucumbers, and all kinds of fruit—melons, dates, figs and pomegranates. Most people ate Roman fashion, reclining at table.

Inns

An Eastern inn, or khan, was not like a modern hotel. Stalls for the travellers to sleep in opened off a central courtyard, where the animals were cared for. The inn-keeper lighted a fire for cooking on and gave fodder to the animals, but travellers had to provide their own food.

Jesus' titles

Lamb of God

John the Baptist described Jesus as the Lamb of God, who took away the sin of the world, reminding his disciples of the lambs used as sacrifices and especially of the lamb killed by each family at Passover festival. When God sent Moses to rescue the people of Israel from Egypt, the Egyptians would not let them leave. Finally Moses, under God's direction, brought about nine terrible disasters upon the land and people. The tenth and last disaster that Moses called down upon them was the death of every firstborn animal and son in one night. By God's instruction, the Israelite families each killed a lamb and sprinkled its blood on their doorpost. God protected their homes from the death that came to every Egyptian family.

Messiah

Messiah is the Hebrew for 'anointed one'. The Greek word is 'Christ'. In Israel, kings, prophets and priests were all anointed with oil at a ceremony dedicating them to God. The people of Israel often referred to their king as 'God's anointed', but they were looking for the promised Messiah who would one day come to reign. Prophets and psalm writers had described this king and many expected a conqueror who would turn out the Romans and give Israel independence. Others longed for a ruler who would bring justice and fairness to poor as well as rich.

Servant of the Lord

The prophet Isaiah called the nation of Israel the servant of the Lord but he also described an obedient, perfect servant who was going to come one day. He would not be proud or overbearing but gentle and quiet. He would suffer and die for his people's sins. It was this picture of the Servant Messiah that Jesus recognized as God's plan for his life—and death.

Son of God

Not everyone expected a Messiah who would be God's Son. Jesus waited for his disciples to discover for themselves that he was more than an ordinary man. Gradually they realized that no mere man could do the things that Jesus did, or make the claims he made.

Son of man

Jesus called himself 'Son of man'. It was a title found in the Book of Daniel to describe someone Daniel saw in a vision, to whom God gave the right to rule over all humankind. Jesus may have used it because it did not give the crowd the impression of a political conqueror.

Jewish leaders

Pharisees

The word means 'separated ones'. Pharisees kept themselves apart from ordinary people by their strictness in keeping every tiny law that had been added to God's law given to Moses. These mostly had to do with outward rules about washing hands and pots and pans in a certain way. Pharisees also fasted twice a week.

Sadducees

The Sadducees belonged to the priestly families and were usually wealthy and aristocratic. They were powerful and managed to get on with their Roman masters. They accepted only the first five books of the Old Testament as Scripture. They did not believe in a life after death.

Scribes

Scribes were generally Pharisees. They spent their time studying the law and all the additions to it that had become part of their tradition. They explained these laws to the people and decided how they should be carried out.

Rabbis

The Hebrew word means 'my teacher' or 'my master'. Pupils called their teacher 'Rabbi'. Scribes were also called rabbi.

Teachers of the Law

See Scribes

Priests, High Priest

Priests were descended from Aaron, the first priest, part of the tribe, or clan, of Levi. There were so many of them in Jesus' day that they took turns to serve in the temple, offering sacrifices and burning incense. The leading priests and the High Priest himself were Sadducees, and had most of the political power in Israel.

Law of Moses

God gave Moses many different laws to help and guide his people. The Ten Commandments have to do with loving God and loving other people. These are lasting laws. There were many other detailed laws concerned with showing fairness and kindness to others. There were also laws about food and cleanliness, to protect the people from disease at that time. The first five books of the Bible, sometimes known as the Books of Moses, contain these laws, as well as many stories.

Levites

Levites belonged to the priests' tribe of Levi, but were not descended from Aaron's family. They helped the priests in their duties.

Salvation

When the angel told Joseph to call Mary's baby Jesus, he explained that it was because the name—'God saves'—would come true. Jesus would save people from the effects of their sins. Many looked for a Messiah who would save the nation by victory in war, as bygone men and women had done in Israel. Jesus brought a more important kind of salvation for people of all races and nations.

Sanhedrin

The Sanhedrin, or Council, was the ruling Jewish court in Jerusalem. It was made up of seventy leading men, Sadducees and Pharisees, plus the High Priest, as chairman. The Romans allowed the Sanhedrin to try and pass sentences. In the case of the death sentence it seems that the Roman authorities had to agree to the charge and carry out the execution.

Satan

Satan, or the Devil, was created by God but rebelled against him. Just as God works for human good, so Satan tries to bring evil and unhappiness. He has his demons, or evil spirits, to help him. He is not God and cannot overcome God's power.

Taxes and tithes

There were hundreds of different taxes and duties to be paid in Jesus' time. Tax collectors made a good profit by charging as much as they dared and pocketing the extra. Jews hated the foreign taxes and looked down on those who collected them. Every Jew paid an annual temple tax, to help towards the upkeep and running of the temple. He also gave a tithe, or tenth, of all his goods or money, as a sign of thankfulness to God. Tithes were paid to the Levites, for their salary. They themselves tithed these gifts and that tithe went to support the priests.

Index